The Challenge
of the Scriptures

FAITH MEETS FAITH

An Orbis Series in Interreligious Dialogue

Paul F. Knitter, General Editor

In our contemporary world, the many religions and spiritualities stand in need of greater intercommunication and cooperation. More than ever before, they must speak to, learn from, and work with each other, in order to maintain their own identity and vitality and so to contribute to fashioning a better world.

FAITH MEETS FAITH seeks to promote interreligious dialogue by providing an open forum for the exchanges between and among followers of different religious paths. While the series wants to encourage creative and bold responses to the new questions of pluralism confronting religious persons today, it also recognizes the present plurality of perspectives concerning the methods and content of interreligious dialogue.

This series, therefore, does not want to endorse any one school of thought. By making available to both the scholarly community and the general public works that represent a variety of religious and methodological viewpoints, FAITH MEETS FAITH hopes to foster and focus the emerging encounter among the religions of the world.

Already published:

FAITH MEETS FAITH SERIES

The Challenge of the Scriptures

The Bible and the Qur'ān

Muslim-Christian Research Group

*Translated from the French
by Stuart E. Brown*

ORBIS BOOKS

Maryknoll, New York 10545

The Catholic Foreign Mission Society of America (Maryknoll) recruits and trains people for overseas missionary service. Through Orbis Books, Maryknoll aims to foster the international dialogue that is essential to mission. The books published, however, reflect the opinions of their authors and are not meant to represent the official position of the society.

ISBN 0-88344-651-0
     0-88344-650-2 (pbk.)

Table of Contents

Acknowledgments

The bold pioneer spirit and excellent teamwork of the Groupe de Recherche Islamo-Chrétien (GRIC) has for several years been an outstanding model to persons interested in serious interfaith encounter. Many such people, however, have been unable to share fully in the excitement occasioned by GRIC's work, because their access to the French language was inadequate to the task of following the intricacies of argument necessary to the elaboration of studies of this type. It was a great honor to be entrusted with the translation of this book on scriptures, and I wish to record my deep appreciation of the confidence of Michel Lelong, Jacques Lévrat and other colleagues for their proposal and unflagging support; I shall never lose the sense of privilege which they have given me by entrusting me with their superb work.

I am indebted to the thoroughness and patience of Michael Fitzgerald, who read the entire draft of this rendering, making valuable observations and suggesting many ingenious emendations, even when he knew that I would not accept them all. I benefited as well from several conversations with Tariq Mitri, who is preparing the Arabic version of the same volume, as we mused together over the nuances of the committee's collective French.

It can be very useful to be married to an editor, especially one who is familiar with the subject at hand and the languages in play. Margaret Brown produced several revisions of the English text, and made numerous helpful comments to improve it. To her, and to our firstborn, Kevin, ever eager to enhance our word-processing skills, I am profoundly grateful.

Finally, I thank the folks at Orbis, especially Eve Drogin, the Senior Editor, and Paul Knitter, the series editor of Faith Meets Faith, for their interest and cooperation. They have made available to the English-reading public one of the major contributions to constructive interfaith dialogue of the late twentieth century, and I am sure that they will have no regrets.

It seems somehow pretentious to dedicate a translation, but I would like to conclude where I began, with a hearty salute to the members of GRIC, and my prayerful best wishes for a *bonne continuation!*

March 1989   *Stuart E. Brown*

Introduction

This volume is the fruit of a research project undertaken between 1978 and 1982 by GRIC (Groupe de Recherches Islamo-Chrétien, or Muslim-Christian Research Group). The group was formed in 1977 at the instigation of a small number of Christian and Muslim colleagues who wanted to work together in meetings and a common research effort in the framework of a Muslim-Christian dialogue.[2]

What is now called dialogue between the two religions has a long history, as we all know, beginning with the birth of Islam in the seventh century. (We even find its echos in the text of the Qur'ān.) But this history over thirteen centuries, for all its occasional moments of illumination and cultural exchange, is essentially made up of polemical and military confrontation, sustained principally by political rivalry between the Christian and Islamic worlds.

Over the past twenty years, in spite of some collusion between religious and socio-political events, the climate has considerably changed. The spread of a planetary civilization based on human achievements has caused even the most homogeneous societies to open up, while population movements have led men and women to discover other, different persons. To recognize such differences is not always easy, but it is inescapable.

Despite some rigidity here and there (not without interest as an important reaction), religions have lost their former preeminence in some societies and ceased to motivate many citizens. Many believers have been led to a new analysis of the fundamentals of their faith and a critical examination of their own religious tradition. Such analyses and examinations cannot be done in a vacuum. Different religious traditions are also coming to understand that they can do better than claim an absolute and exclusive possession of the truth: they should share their faith, common and different, and seek fresh ways of presenting their spiritual heritage to the men and women of our time.

The past few years have also experienced a virtually spontaneous blossoming of meetings between Christians and Muslims both in the historic Christian lands and in Muslim areas. These meetings have been at every level imaginable, from simple everyday life through informal friendship groups to international colloquia. This development, which is substantially

1

new, is without doubt one of the signs or "graces" of our era. But we must not harbor any illusions: the vast majority of Christian and Muslim believers feel little interest in opening to others. They are preoccupied by daily cares or by the internal problems of their community, even when they no longer continue to defend their besieged "fortress."

Increasingly frequent and much in the media's attention, international colloquia (Córdoba, 1974, 1977; Tunis, 1974, 1979, 1982, 1986; Tripoli, 1976, to mention just a few)[3] have certainly helped to make public opinion more aware of a new attitude of encounter between religions that were formerly turned in on themselves. The meetings have allowed, and continue to allow, leaders and researchers to become acquainted and sometimes to form lasting friendships. They touch on basic questions that concern our religions in their convergences and their differences, or that bring them together before the challenges of the modern world. But the public nature and the more or less official mandate given the delegates to these colloquia—or at least the mandate they often assume—have an unavoidable impact on their deliberations. It is very easy to slip into apologetics and there have been instances of rather vehement polemic. In the best of cases, the system of successive addresses prepared beforehand gives rise to "parallel speeches" that rarely converge and leave little space for deep discussion.

GRIC was born of such experiences, even as it sought to be different. Indeed, it is not (only) a Muslim-Christian friendship group like so many others. Nor is it a colloquium of experts from the two religions, nor a research center with official members, such as we know in many countries. Meeting on an equal footing, some Christian and Muslim friends, trained in the requirements of scientific research and having a serious knowledge of their own religious tradition and its current problems as well as an adequate familiarity with the other tradition, decided to work together to propose new directions. They did this without any official mandate but in the full solidarity of their faith communities. Such were the basic elements of the project that developed over time and determined the nature of the group.

The private character[4] of the participation of each person—which excludes any mandate, official or informal, that could involve religious or political authorities—seemed to us indispensable in order to assure freedom of research. But we do not intend by this to cut ourselves off from our religious communities or hierarchies. On the contrary, we explicitly affirm that we are believers in full solidarity with our respective faith communities and we consciously assume the heritage of our religious traditions, reserving nonetheless the right to look at them critically. We do not want to be snipers separated from our communities. Our group is private, but never closed. Everyone who is interested in the research may share in it, in one form or another. The only conditions are the acceptance of the basic guidelines and the capacity to make a positive contribution to our work, even if this is only in the form of constructive criticism.

This basic point of independence was hotly debated during our first general meetings. We feel that it is simply the modern translation of traditional Islamic and Christian teachings. In Islam, it is the principle of *ijtihād*, the right of personal reflection, which is given to any Muslim adequately trained in religious science. As for Christianity, or at least Roman Catholicism, noted for its concern for doctrinal security and hierarchic authority in matters of faith, the Second Vatican Council has repeatedly recognized that theologians have full freedom of research, under the supervision of the magisterium.

But it is only the serious quality of research and the coherence of its conclusions that can confer any authority. It is in this sense that we have tried to work, eager to open new avenues without claiming any representativity—a very ambiguous notion in any case—and without directly committing our communities.

The other criteria of participation raise fewer problems. A modern university background is necessary to allow cooperation according to a common method and with a common concern for criticism and objectivity, excluding as far as possible any prejudices or prior conditions.

Technical competence is necessary on two levels: first, participants must be sufficiently aware not only of their own religious tradition but also of the other. Thus, the Christian must be able to discuss any particular subject not only in terms of Christian doctrine, but of Islamic doctrine as well, and vice versa. Of course, the members of one religion are to authenticate, criticize, or contest what those of another say about it, and they must be heard. The second level of technical competence refers to the chosen theme of study, so that the composition of the group is likely to vary—and in fact has varied—according to the theme under study. There are no permanent members in the strict sense of the term. However, during eight years of working together, especially in the several local sections that generally met once a month, strong relationships have been woven among the members so that a substantial continuity has been in evidence in the composition of the sections from one theme to another. Nevertheless, the principle of mobility remains in force.

Finally, a climate of friendship is necessary for a free and frank exchange, without aggression and without polemic. One can only be frank among friends. Moreover, this group could not have been formed if some Muslims and some Christians had not already had a long experience of mutual friendship. It could not have continued and deepened its work if this friendship that allowed total freedom and sincerity had not also continued to develop. In any case, is this not the basic law of all true dialogue? The exchanges of words and ideas bear truth and light only if the interlocutors have invested themselves and their lives in a communion of friendship in order to invest them in their word.

We feel that GRIC, thus defined, has its place, original and without doubt necessary, in the variegated setting of contemporary Christian-Muslim relationships.

THE BEGINNINGS OF THE STUDY OF SCRIPTURE

The real start came in the spring of 1976, after the Muslim-Christian dialogue seminar in Tripoli, Libya (February 1–6). This was doubtless the most representative colloquium of its kind, with regard to its scope and its limitations. Some of us thought that another sort of meeting was both possible and desirable. After a year's reflection, some fifteen persons from a variety of countries gathered during a free period in the November 1977 Judeo-Muslim-Christian colloquium at Sénanque Abbey (Vaucluse, France). A preparatory "Proposal for a Muslim-Christian Research Group" had been circulated beforehand, and served as the basis for the initial charter, *General Orientations for a Dialogue in Truth*. This text, after a word-by-word examination, was revised and enlarged at the 1978 Sénanque gathering. It appears in full following the present "Introduction."[5]

From the several topics suggested in the "Proposal," the theme of scripture, Word of God, and the fundamental scriptures of our religions seemed of prime importance, in spite of the competition of topics like "Faith and Politics." Indeed, the interpretation of scripture is one of the keys, and even the most important among them, that allow our "scriptural" religions to bring the light of the Word of God to human problems. Moreover, the mutual recognition of our respective scriptures raises serious questions that are at the heart of the friction between our religious traditions, and which have not as yet received an adequate reply.

Once this theme had been chosen, a list was prepared of individual Muslims and Christians who might participate in a research project on scripture and who would also fit the criteria for belonging to GRIC as defined in the *General Orientations*, which is to say academics trained to work on the texts and especially exegetes and theologians; sixteen of them each wrote a personal appreciation of Christian and Muslim doctrines of scripture. These personal contributions provided the basis for a synthesis prepared by two editors, one Christian and one Muslim. This report was sent to eighteen persons (nine from each community), and of these fifteen met at Sénanque in September 1978 to discuss the synthesis and lay the groundwork for future research.

This meeting also provided the occasion for structuring GRIC in local sections in various countries, by assigning each section a particular aspect of the theme. The Paris group took charge of general questions: Word of God, reading, scripture. The Algeria section was to study Christian and Muslim exegeses. The Rabat branch would concentrate on the ways in which scripture is currently received by believers and by communities. The scholars in Tunis would try to find ways toward a recognition by the followers of one faith of the other's scripture: a Christian view of the Qur'ān, a Muslim view of the Bible. A coordinating secretary based in Paris would watch over general developments, while the two editors would continue to be generally available. Each section was to prepare an annual report a month before the general meeting so that everyone could study it beforehand. It was agreed that some twenty persons would attend each annual general meeting, divided equally between the two faith groups. It seemed to us that a larger number would make it difficult to have a full and deep exchange of opinion. Each section was to delegate its representatives to the annual meeting.

There were thus twenty-one persons at the Tunis meeting, September 10–13, 1979, and they held a preliminary study of the Algeria and Rabat reports. They conducted as well an exercise in structural analysis on two passages of the Bible and the Qur'ān.

The 1980 meeting was once again at Sénanque (September 9–12). Much of it was spent on a study of the Paris report, which was rather technical, in order to make it more readable. The Algeria and Rabat documents were again discussed, but no final text was approved.

It was perhaps the Rabat meeting (September 8–11, 1981) that marked the real turning point. After some tense exchanges, often passionate but always friendly, the Christians and Muslims arrived at a formula to express the process of the Word of God in human language (see chap. 1, below, pp. 16ff.).

There remained the final lap, which was no less important than the others: a reassessment of the Qur'ān in terms of the Christian faith, and of the Bible in the light of Islamic faith. This task was entrusted to the Tunis section, which worked at it intensely for four years, developing a voluminous dossier, notably on the historical side. Not without some difficulty, the Tunis section managed to condense its report to 52 pages, and this was the principal subject of the 1982 meeting, held at Korbous near Tunis, September 5–8, 1982. Again, the discussion was ardent, even strained, with occasional moments of suspense. Thanks to some serious effort at reflection and imagination, to a sustained dialogue and to the common will for advancing the work, some original solutions were found.

This meeting was to complete our research on scripture, so we made final revisions to the Paris and Rabat texts. There was still one passage of the Tunis report (on Christian attitudes to the Qur'ān) that needed a definitive rendition, although there was already consensus on the general lines, and this task was given to a small committee. This group could not meet until March 1985, which explains the delay in our publication, but it is finally the text of all our research on scripture, which can be found in the pages of this book.

The Korbous meeting also chose a new theme for our future research: "Secularization: Problems and Risks."

During these years of common research, some major difficulties and even some serious tensions developed. The subject lent itself to this: everyone knows how dear scripture is to the heart and the faith of Christians and Muslims. Moreoever, the approaches to scripture through exegesis, hermeneutics, or simple reading in faith, are quite different in our two traditions, in spite of some points in common. The most profound difference is doubtless the placing of scripture in the process that goes from the Word of God to its reception by the believer.

We feel that we have at least located exactly where this difference lies by speaking, *for Islam* (or for *the Qur'ān*), of a literal tradition and, *for Christianity* (or for *the Bible*), of an interpretive tradition (in the constitution of the actual corpus of scripture), thus opening ways toward a mutual recognition of our authentic scriptures.

However, two points should be stressed. First, it is noteworthy that the confrontations hardly ever arose between Christians and Muslims, whether in local gatherings or the annual general meetings. They involved several spiritual groupings, equally represented in the two religions. The other point is that we always reached a consensus, not through concessions, but by a common deepening of our awareness. Our rules provided for the possibility of setting forth in our conclusions two or more positions on any topic, provisionally insoluble. They also allowed a vote to resolve stalemates. We never had to use either of these procedures.

This text on scripture is thus the faithful rendering of five years of collective work in GRIC, for every portion was discussed during the annual meetings, line by line, sometimes word by word. Each is the result of an explicit consensus, even if some parts would have been treated otherwise by other sections. The disparity among them is indicative of the disparity among the members and sections of GRIC: of the three local sections reponsible for the several portions, one was made up of researchers who were themselves specialists (academic or theological) in linguistic or exegetic research and thus homogenous; another was more broadly formed of academics who were not specialists in these questions, while the third group comprised these two elements in roughly equal parts.

GRIC has evolved over the years. New sections came into being (Brussels in 1980; Paris II in 1981). Conversely, the Algeria section, which had undertaken the study of Christian and Muslim exegesis, had to suspend its operations because of certain difficulties, without finishing its report. Besides, some participants in the early meetings were unable to attend the later ones. In Appendix 1 there is a list of those who contributed to this work, both at local and general levels. In order not to attach responsibility to those who were not with us to the end, we decided to publish in two stages. The definitive version of the complete text was first copied and sent to everyone who had collaborated in the work, however briefly. Everyone was invited to give their personal agreement on the text as it stood, without amendment. But they could also refuse to sign, in which case their name would not appear on the common list. They could also affix their name and express certain comments or reservations on various points or on the full text. We promised to note these; they can be found in Appendix 2.

Since 1982, then, GRIC has been studying secularization. The difficulties surrounding this subject are no less great than for scripture, even though they are of a very different order. This study was completed in 1985, at least in a provisional and sectorial fashion. We hope to offer our conclusions to our readers in a form that has yet to be decided.[6] Since 1985, we have been examining the theme "Faith and Justice."

In spite of many difficulties (and financial problems are not the least of these) GRIC continues.[7] Already in its brief career, it has experienced crises that threatened its breakup, but the will to go on shown by most of those involved in this venture has so far always won the day. New sections have been formed (Beirut, Dakar, Cairo). Responsible religious organizations, both Christian and Muslim, have encouraged our efforts. Even if they do not always adopt our positions officially, they accept the freedom of our quest. The future will tell whether our hopes are sound. Whatever happens, those who have lived through these years of common research will have experienced a deepening of their own faith and a communion with the faith of their partners.

A testimony of our reflection and published as such, the text that follows does not claim to provide the general or official thinking of our faith communities, nor even the last word on our ideas of scripture. Doctrinal reflection in our religions remains open and will conclude only at the end of time. Simply, we have tried to go as far as the current state of our reflection and the capacities of the participants would permit. A solitary thinker, Christian or Muslim, would doubtless have gone further. Many readers will find us quite timid. But it is important to underline, on the one hand, that the contours and significance of our text will appear clearly only to the reader who is already sufficiently familiar with the respective positions of Islam and Christianity on scripture, and the pertinent difficulties; this significance, on the other hand, seems to us to be closely bound to the common character of the research produced. In any case, we have made considerable progress in five years and, even if we have stopped (for the moment, perhaps) our work on scripture, we believe that this text indicates future directions. It is not impossible that GRIC could return to this theme someday, if God grants it the time.

General Guidelines for True Dialogue: Basic Charter of GRIC, Muslim-Christian Research Group

I. FIDELITY TO OUR FAITH AND MUTUAL OPENNESS

1. We, both Christians and Muslims, believe that God has been revealed in the Word. Muslims recognize this revelation in the Qur'ān. Christians see it in Jesus Christ himself, the Word of God made human. Each of our communities believes that its faith is a gift from God accepted by humankind, and that this constitutes for it a very special way of encountering God. It is for this reason that we are Christians or Muslims, not followers of another religion or atheists.

Yet, however perfect may be the Word on which our faith is founded, we do not think that the knowledge we are granted of this Word entirely exhausts its riches or those of the divine mystery. This conviction entails two consequences. On the one hand, the certitude of our faith leads us necessarily, with God's help and with God's light, to an unceasing search for the truth. On the other hand, we are led to recognize that approaches to the truth other than our own, based on a Word different from that on which our faith is founded, are legitimate, and that they can be fruitful for us also.

In other words, the Muslim recognizes the validity and fruitfulness of the faith of Christians, while the Christian recognizes the validity and fruitfulness of the faith of Muslims and of their search for the truth.

2. Within this perspective, each of us remains firmly attached to the essence of our faith and to the outlook on the world implied by it. It is in this light of faith that we wish to situate the religion of our partners in dialogue. We do not, however, require of them that they adopt categories bound up with our own faith outlook. Both Christians and Muslims have to broaden their vision and widen their categories in order to take into account the other tradition's religious value.

Put in clearer terms, this means, for example, that a Christian should not require of Muslims that they adopt the Christian faith in the divinity of Christ, and that Muslims should not require a Christian to recognize the Qur'ān as the final revelation of God's word and Muhammad as the seal of the prophets.

3. This is why we refuse any form of syncretism, for this would only tend to obscure essential differences between our two religions. Yet all too often these differences are kept in the foreground, and sometimes our religions are seen to be opposed on the grounds of differences that do not really exist. Our aim is not to do away with the essential differences, nor to minimize them, nor to pass them over in silence. Rather do we wish to recognize them in complete loyalty, and to situate them in their rightful place.

4. This is also the reason why we are not trying to reconcile the irreconcilable. We are not seeking to suppress or to minimize our essential differences, or to find some common denominator that would reconcile oppositions only at the price of truth. Our aim is to define exactly where essential divergences really lie, not where they are thought to lie when envisaged from the standpoint of fixed systems. Convinced as we are that the points of convergence between our respective creedal outlooks are more numerous and more important than they are generally thought to be, we feel that by underlining these we shall throw a sharper light on the really fundamental differences.

Respect for the irreconcilable holds good also for the members of our group, for both Christians among themselves and Muslims among themselves. It is not to be supposed in advance that each side will be unanimous on all points. It is only normal that divergent opinions, on questions of greater or lesser importance, should be expressed by participants belonging to the same religion. Our discussions together may help to bring these opinions closer together, or even to bring them into agreement. But differences may remain that could only be eliminated by doing violence to conscience or by adopting compromise solutions. Rejecting such false ways at the outset, we shall make an honest record of these differences that cannot for the moment be reconciled and we shall mention them in the texts we publish.

II. REPRESENTATIVITY

We reject in advance the objection that the members of our group, and the results of our research, do not represent the way of thinking of the majority in the religious communities to which we belong.

In point of fact, from the very first moment that we envisaged setting up this Christian-Muslim research group, we agreed that members would belong to it in their private capacities and not as persons mandated by some religious or political authority. We engage in this work as believers; resolved to remain completely faithful to the sources of our faith, critically aware that we are heirs to centuries-old traditions, in full and unreserved solidarity with our respective faith communites. Yet we are at the same time believers who are striving for a better understanding of their faith, who seek to respond to the demands of the present world, and thus to contribute to progress in our communities. This is why we shall undertake to publish our investigations. By so doing, all those whose interest is aroused by our approach and by the results we achieve will be able to evaluate them and, eventually, to contribute to them by their criticism. The seriousness of our research will be the sole guarantee to which we shall appeal for the validity of our conclusions.

III. OPENNESS TO CRITICISM FROM OUTSIDE

1. All of us, both Christians and Muslims, accept the way our partners of the other religion present their faith, both to themselves and to us. Our era, however, is characterized by the encounter of different cultures. This being so, each of us is led to make a fresh analysis of the foundations of our faith, and to examine in a critical fashion the way in which our religious tradition has evolved. This can no longer be attempted in isolation. Openness to mutual criticism is one of the requirements of our age. We come to true self-knowledge only if we take into account how others see us. This is why we want to know how others see us, whether they belong to another religion or to none, whether they are believers or not. We are open both to questions and critical remarks, provided always that these do not spring from an apologetical or polemical attitude.

2. This holds good within our research group also. One of its basic principles is that members must not know only their own religion but should be sufficiently familiar with the other religion as well. In personal contribution each should cover both the Christian and Muslim positions on any particular question. Yet experience has shown that, generally speaking, each of us tends to understand the other religion according to its classical formulations, without paying sufficient attention to more recent positions. Christianity and Islam, however, are both living religions. Current thinking must therefore guide our reflection. We cannot be content to consider only the classical formulations for each religion. Thus, when a member of the group puts forward some position that he or she has been led to adopt after serious reflection, we must be ready to accept this, although we may wish to ask for an explanation of the reasons for adopting this position, and we may wish to offer our own criticism of it.

IV. WE DO NOT OWN THE PRINCIPLES OF OUR FAITH

We do not think that the divine Word, the foundation of our faith, belongs exclusively to us, whether we be Christians or Muslims. Christian faith is based on the person of Jesus and the witness of the Apostles' faith as contained in the New Testament. But the historical phenomenon of Jesus of Nazareth and the texts of the New Testament writings are facts and documents available for investigation by all. Similarly Islamic faith is based on the Qur'ān and the authentic tradition of the Prophet. But the qur'anic text and the life of Muhammad b. 'Abdallâh form part of the general history of the human race and belong to its spiritual heritage.

This is why on both sides, with regard to the historical facts that ground our faith and with regard to our scriptures, we accept "readings" other than our own. Such "readings" can be based simply on the human sciences or they can take their origin in a faith other than our own, which may or may not make use of a scientific approach. In this way there can be a Christian or an agnostic "reading" of the Qur'ān, a Muslim or agnostic "reading" of the New Testament.

V. FRATERNITY IN FAITH

These days faith in God is challenged from all sides and in many different ways. We think that all religions together have to face up to these challenges. But this is particularly the duty of Christianity and Islam. This means that Christians and Muslims have to reply together to the challenges coming from within and without. This in no way implies that we should band together as believers in a "common front" to wage a dialectical or political war against those who voice these challenges. What is required of us is rather a constant effort to overcome the politico-religious oppositions that have in the past led to conflict. The oppositions belong to a situation that should be superceded, a situation in which no distinctions are made between faith, religion, society, and temporal power. We believers have to get together. Together as believers we must confront the challenges of the world today. We will then be able to help our respective communities to derive some benefit from questions raised by these challenges. We shall be able to help them to propose suitable answers to them. In this way the light and hope that our communities bear may come to be recognized and accepted by all who are seeking justice and peace.

Muslims, whether Sunnis, Shi'ites or Kharijites, recognize each other first of all as Muslims. Similarly Christians, whether Catholics, Orthodox, Anglicans, or Protestants, recognize each other now, first of all, as Christians, "followers of Christ." In the same way Christians and Muslims should recognize each other first of all as believers, "followers of faith in God." The term "interreligious ecumenism," understood in this way, quite aptly describes, we feel, the aspirations of our group.

VI. ABSENT VOICES

Some persons may be surprised to see our group composed of Christians and Muslims only, without anyone representing the other great religious or nonreligious ideologies. The absence of anyone to represent Judaism will be particularly noticeable. We wish to restate here what our group has said ever since it began working. Our Christian-Muslim dialogue will not be conducted in isolation. It will be characterized by openness to the other great religions and ideologies found in the world today. Given the framework of our reflection—monotheistic faith—we would sincerely wish our Jewish believers to be present. The circumstances of our time (the Palestine question, which arises inevitably in every meeting bringing together Jews, Christians, and Muslims) and problems of practical organization (it is easier to start a dialogue between two groups only) have led us to limit our meetings to Christians and Muslims. Yet we keep alive the ardent hope that in the future a wider dialogue will be possible.

—translated by Michael Fitzgerald,
Islamochristiana, 6 (1980): 230–33

1

Word of God —
Holy Writ and Reading

Treating complementary aspects of the fact of scripture, this part of our study examines how the Word of God became scripture, how it was handed down and read. The text is the result of the work of the first Paris group, and was presented in a more technical form at the annual assembly in Sénanque (1980). It was discussed and revised for the assemblies held in Rabat (1981) and Tunis-Korbous (1982).

THE INITIAL EVENT AND ITS OBJECTIFICATIONS

In this first section we seek to elaborate a model that could be suitable for both Islam and Christianity. We find in these two scriptural societies, three basic elements defining the field of religious production, whether textual or institutional: an initial event, an original text, and an exegetic community with its particular rules of operation.

We shall first reflect on the relationship between the "initial event" and the Word of God itself. We shall then see just how this initial event must be subjected to historical objectifications, whether in the form of scripture or in the form of institutional structures.

Word of God and Revelational Event

1. The very notion of an "initial event" is somewhat difficult. A "scientific" approach would consider it as the believing community's reconstruction of its own origins in the socio-historical idiom of a given age. But in a context of belief, the initial event can and must be understood as the intervention of the "Word of God" in human history. As religious traditions, Christianity and Islam make sense only as they relate to the specific event by which the Word of God became present in the life and thought of human beings in history. We shall speak generally of the "Christ-event" to which the earliest Christian community bears witness and in which we must in-

clude his life, his work, and his message. And we shall refer to the "Qur'ān-event," as it was experienced, transmitted, and explained by the Prophet.

2. It would be illusory to try to contrast Islam with Christianity as though the former was a religion of the book and the latter a religion based on a historic event. *Each* of them refers to a founding event. But it is essential to see that this source-event itself sends us back to an absent origin, the very Word of God or even the divine will to communicate with humankind. In the context of belief, faith alone can discern the presence of God in this inaugural event, which each believing community experiences as a Word from God. But this inaugural event belongs in fact to ordinary history, and is therefore included in a socio-historical system wherein we can identify the material and ideological interests that conditioned its advent.

3. What we conventionally call "revelation" consists first in the transcendent Word of God becoming an object of awareness for human intelligence. The initial event is already experienced as "the Word of God" by the believing community. But one can speak of revelation only in the strict sense when this initial event evokes a *witness*, which in turn becomes a *scripture*. The scripture is the middle term (graphic materialization) by which the eternal Word of God becomes a Word of God for humans. The process of revelation is thus inseparably history and scripture, and it is this whole set of phenomena that constitutes "the initial event": that is, the primary and recurrent reference from which each religious tradition draws life.

4. If we consider the full historical impact of the initial revelatory event, we can say that the expression "Word of God" can be understood on three levels. First of all, there is the Word of God as an originating event: it is the very act of God's speaking by which God communicates with humans. Next, there is the Word of God as an occurrence: this is the advent of the Word of God through the mediation of history and prophetic witness. There is, finally, the Word of God as scripture: the biblical canon, the book of the Qur'ān.

This calls us to underline the lack of equivalence between the inaccessible referent of the Word of God and its objectifications in history or in scripture. Revelation has its source in the unspeakable mystery of God. This is why any attempt to render absolute the letter of the sacred text as if it was the very Word of God without intermediary is a surrendering of the ineffable character of the transcendent Word of God.

Textual Objectifications of the Word of God

1. Revelation is always *indirect*. That is to say, there is no immediate revelation in the sense of divine words pronounced by God. In other words, revelation is always the Word of God in human language. God neither speaks nor writes as humans do. But God calls persons who transmit the Word in God's Name. The "theandric" character of the Word of God has

allowed Christian thought to see in the prophetic revelation of the Old Testament a preparation for the incarnation. And even in the case of Jesus Christ, who is, in the eyes of Christian faith, the eternal Word of God made human, his humanity is radically human and expresses itself in human language. In the case of the Qur'ān, which is, in the eyes of Muslim faith, the Word of God, this Word expresses itself in human language in the Arabic tongue of the society of the time of the Prophet and his companions.

2. There is a textual objectification of the Word of God to the extent that the prophetic Word as an actualization of the sense of the initial event becomes a scripture. Scripture, as a deposit of prophetic witness, is itself a witness. To witness, in fact, is to endow the word put forth by the Prophet with the status of a divine Word. In doing this, we promote the text to a new existence. It is impossible to dissociate the initial event from the new meaning it acquires through witness. And it is the scripture that shows us clearly what occurs in witness as a word directly related to the event.

3. It is thus possible to say that scripture as a textual objectification of the Word of God is a witness marked by the whole historical fabric of a believing community, subject to its own needs of legitimization and identification. For Christians, as a result, the word "tradition" means something more than the simple history of rereading the original text within the believing community. It also indicates a process within scripture itself. In the Old Testament, for example, it is the manner in which Israel heard and reinterpreted the events of its history as an alliance with God. It is also the manner in which the first Christian community heard and reinterpreted the event of Jesus of Nazareth. In the case of Islam, we do not perceive a similar distance between the qur'anic utterances of the Prophet, memorized by the companions who afterward assembled them with the object of establishing the *"mushaf"* (definitive official corpus). It will be recognized, however, that an awareness of the socio-historical context in which the Qur'ān was revealed is necessary for an understanding of its meaning.

4. Whether we are considering the New Testament or the text of the Qur'ān, we must understand them as the *testimonies* of the first community assembled by Jesus or Muhammad. Far from being an obstacle, the most serious possible attention to the historical distance that separates us from these early testimonies is the essential condition for a living interpretation today. Every new reading, historically conditioned, creates meaning. There is no question of reading the text as though the letter exhausted the fulness of the Word of God. Nor is there any claim to become contemporary with the meaning of the Prophet. It is simply a matter of producing in community a fresh realization of the text in full continuity with the foundational wording. We may speak of a correlation of functions between the original text and its realization, ever new, in the respective relationships to a given socio-historical context. And, today as yesterday, we cannot explain the function of the text for the faith community without considering the broad socio-historical context in which it is found.

Institutional Objectifications of the Word of God

In every religious society based on an inaugural event, there is thus of necessity a textual objectification of this event. The "text" is the only means to becoming contemporary with the initial event, which in turn sends us back to the transcendent mystery of God. That is to say that there is no relationship to God on the basis of an inaugural event without a confession of faith and without a whole process of religious idealization and historical action. The "original text" gradually gives birth to an "ideological stock," which is in fact a collection of rereadings, glosses, commentaries, and normative texts. It is in relationship to this entire process that we must understand the need for an institutional objectification.

1. Indeed, within every living religion that seeks to maintain its identity through the social transformations of the surrounding world, the so-called textual production is perforce accompanied by an *institutional* production. That objectification restricts the system of historical action. For those in authority, it always harks back to the founder's message. It exercises a function of *legitimation* and *reproduction* for the faith group in its exchanges with other symbolic systems and other systems of social organization. There is a necessary reciprocal interaction between the faith group in its own originality and its socio-historical environment. A given religion may be at the roots of a new social structuration. But conversely, however loyal it may be to its origins, we cannot understand the historical evolution of a religion without an appreciation of its role in the dominant culture and the prevailing system of social organization.

2. This necessary institutional objectification will vary with each historical religion or system of action. But it always involves institutions to regulate and define articles of faith.

In the case of Christianity, faith in Jesus Christ as messenger of God was entrusted to the apostles and the first disciples. In the beginning, the "rule of faith" or "rule of truth" was nothing but the preaching by the apostles of the Christ-event in the context of the biblical tradition. Afterward, two principal instances of regulation were imposed, although it is difficult to say precisely when or where: the ministry of the college of bishops, which was meant to extend the initial mission of the college of apostles (which became the magisterium within Roman Catholicism, and the councils and synods within Protestantism), and the regulatory pronouncements of theologians.

In the case of Islam, the disciples of the Prophet formed a small community that sought to apply the qur'anic precepts with reference to the prophetic teachings that explained them. But with the rapid expansion of Islam and the emergence of new problems requiring homogeneous solutions in conformity with a logic discernible over time and space, the need for specialization in religious sciences became evident. Thus there gradually developed a particular social class, which the Muslim community recognized as competent in qur'anic exegesis, jurisprudence, and the transmission of *hadith*. Rules were made—later to be clothed in theories for the sciences of the origins of religion and of law—to define the limits that could not be overstepped in order to ensure the perpetuation of the system, but with sufficient internal freedom of interpretation.

3. The function of the authorities instituted within a faith group, whether Islam or Christianity, consists of proclaiming the permanence of an original message faithfully transmitted, and requiring a constant application in all its fulness. In concrete terms, the ecclesiastical authorities or the *'ulamā* came in fact to possess the virtual power of defining orthodoxy at the level of the beliefs and practices of the community of faith. According to Roman Catholic convictions, these authorities have, through the will of the founder, a normative power of interpretation. In Islam as in Protestantism, "clerks" are not theoretically mandated by anyone to exercise this power. Historically, however, the office assigned to clerks can usurp in any context an inordinate power over truth. Indeed it tends to continue the line that legitimates its monopoly as the sole authentic interpreter, rejecting any innovation as marginal or deviant. Its power is armed with a variety of instruments for imposing its will. Some of these are of a judicial nature, while others depend on psychological persuasion. Those who assume this role can thus censure, punish, exclude, or readmit the members of its faith group.

4. Whether or not it adopts an orthodox or revisionist critical form, the thinking of the clerks (theologians, exegetes, jurists, *uṣūlīyun*, fundamentalists, and others) can fulfill its function only in the framework of a socio-historical context. Its symbolic production must be judged in the knowledge that it operates within several constraints besides those of faith, even when it seeks simply to affirm its own legitimacy and credibility. Its relationship to the original message will necessarily be determined by its relationship with the institution that would perpetuate it. Such was the situation in history of any idea that was satisfied merely to explain and elaborate official doctrine. But there has also always been an essentially critical theological function trying to produce an explanation of the faith that would take into account the real needs of believers confronted with cultural displacement and social transformation. Thus, what we call theology can either help to articulate the message in a more intelligible way or sink into the status of an ideology in the service of the powerful.

SCRIPTURE IS ALSO A *BOOK*

Many faith communities are conditioned by a foundational book, the religious status of which may vary. In every case, nevertheless, there exists, objectively speaking, *a book*: a real book, which can be the object of extreme reverence as well as something to be sold in a bookshop; a book that like any text—which of course it is, primarily—can be subject to differing approaches and open to the broadest range of readings across time, space, and culture, both within and beyond the faith community.[1]

If, with reference to the transcendent, the theologian says whence the book "comes," we, at the level of analysis we have chosen, seek only to say what it "does." This allows us to use the same tools in our linguistically and culturally diverse societies—and we shall not forget that some of these are more oral than literal—and so to ensure the basis of a common inquiry.

Apart from any other theological problem about the means of revelation or the plan of God, or more directly about the fact of the Qur'ān or the Bible, we have at this objective level to acknowledge the reality of the book, of its material existence as a text received and recognized as scripture in our communities, and also in the human societies to which it has been sent.

A book is a product that has appeared and circulated, that has been received and transmitted within a given society; it is from this angle that we can analyze the transition from the original treatise to the status of a text.

The founding book of a faith community, which is the heir of a given socio-cultural legacy, never ceases to appear to be both congruent with this society and at the same time subversive. Assuming the idiom that will make it intelligible, it also serves a novel and critical articulation, which is perceived as a breach corresponding to an attack by something entirely alien or absolutely new, which can be termed eschatological. It provokes a fundamental questioning of schematic structures and established policies, because it suggests new models.

It is audible but at the same time considered to be "unheard of" and loaded, as a basic idiom, with a whole series of possibilities to be discovered and put into practice. What would without it have been only a diffuse eschatological imagining, becomes real and instrumental, and finds its own operational form.

If, then, we only take things at the level of the book-object (something produced) in the society that recognizes it to be scripture, we have adopted the mode of appropriation that would best allow us to discern the book's social functions. The range of possibilities is quite broad and a typology must still be developed. We shall outline this in our third section.

Thus, whether we are dealing with the Bible, which was the fruit of a long process of canonization, or the Qur'ān, which appeared in definitive form soon after the proclamation of the directly received founding revelation, the requisite transition from an oral to a scriptural format is a decisive operation, wherein we register the imprints, faint in places but indelible, of this original moment in the life of our text. These imprints are the signs of the dynamic effectiveness of the initial discourse as it blazes its trail, over and around the tensions born of the powers in place at the time of its appearance in history.

DIFFERENT READINGS OF THE BOOK

We have thus taken into account the emergence of the book within the society that has identified with it: no satisfactory analysis could be limited to the reconstitution of an original oral discourse, however close it came to the received text; neither could there be any adequate familiarity with the definitive state of the book that failed to note within it and elsewhere the traces of the story of its advent.

The fact that the book is the object of readings constitutes another angle of approach: language, which is itself a call for reading, while its composition or texture raises a set of possibilities for reading that give structure to the scriptural society. Analysis will avail itself of all the linguistic sciences, from philology to those investigations that penetrate the depths of enunciation,[2] in order to illuminate an initial internal dialogue in the text itself, a sort of self-interpretation by the book; we can already see the incessant interplay of readings and rereadings, which somehow wrap the text at hand inside the consciousness of the scriptural society.

The difficulty and the richness of the exegesis of the book, whether authorized or not, are in relation to the growing complexity of this context of readings and interpretive testimonies that comprise it or that it engenders.

Even if we take for granted a sure and considerable historical documentation, we must still dissect the structure of the corpus of received interpretations, which are mostly normative. The semantic matrix bears the marks of the permanent encounter between the irreducible originality of the book's message and everything that makes a social human being: his or her religious aspirations, psychological states, and various forces, notably those that manifest themselves during the expansion of communities of the book or the ideological tautness that corresponds to periods of defensiveness.[3]

In terms of a contribution to the discussion of exegetic questions, we cannot do more now than attempt a typology that would allow us an exchange free of misunderstanding when we eventually undertake a common analysis.

Three major tendencies can be distinguished in the approaches that most evidently influence the structuring of a hermeneutic or "symbol capital" within the scriptural society. At different levels and according to the immense variety of techniques ranging from the selective memorization of certain fragments of the book to the most elaborate exegesis, these approaches may be apprehended in the no less varied circumstances of access to the text.[4]

1. The first type of readings that the scriptural society encounters could be termed *archeological*: exegesis must indicate the original meaning, the absolutely normative beginnings. In the attempt, it seeks to establish a continuity of reading by reducing the conflicts in interpretation to a binary system of true and false meanings. Although it often musters a vast array of technical equipment for linguistic and historical investigation, this sort of exegesis is actually quite close to the "innocent" readings that eagerly claim an inspired or intuitive proximity to "the" meaning of the text and it can even keep track of them within the community. This reading usually

seeks to fill the role of direct critic in opposition to hermeneutic renewal within the scriptural society.

2. A second type would *resolve the finality of the text by decoding its historical effects:* endowed with a graph of reading and history, it develops models to which it ascribes a certain factual hermeneutic. The degree of elaboration can, here also, vary considerably: the existence of "spiritual beings" would seem to verify the capacity of the message to convert persons to the faith; the scientific revolution would confirm the liberating impulse of the scriptures, and so on. More or less subject to the constraints of a serene appreciation of history, this approach remains retrospective: it draws the unstated elements of the text from the interpretations of the past in order to discover its permanent function. It often vindicates an established value system, but it also forces the society to notice the concrete impact of the fact of reading, making it aware of its continuity with the initial community.

3. A third approach basically expects the current confrontation with the received text as source and object of tradition to produce *the expression of an original meaning today*; that is to say, new and constituting an emerging state of society. Readings of this type have an eschatological thrust.

Instead of perpetuating the meaning, exegesis here assumes the task of discerning a totally innovative meaning of the text, which is understood to be revelatory; that is, actively revealing the society to itself under the liberating shock of the message. The founding discourse, original in time and taken fully into account by the two types of exegesis described earlier, now engenders a discourse that is both unhoped-for and expected, and its irruption jostles afresh the latent state of the religious society.

These three types of reading, which correspond to the social functions of the text, combine with one another and mingle their effects so thoroughly that any attempt at a critical analysis of these readings may be suspected by the faith group as liable to "break" something. It is not unusual, strangely, for it to attribute this feeling to the book itself and to live through the experience as a sacrilege, confusing readings with the text, before reaching via this detour a way of access to the freedom of the message.

In fact, any reading is both revelatory and inadequate. Even the most "naive" are like this, although they may appear to be more innocent than others. This is why scriptural societies have always appropriated the best tools available in the conceptual apparatus of any period in order to distinguish among modes of reading, even at the risk of endorsing opposing views in differing circumstances. There exists an educational dialectic between contrasting types of reading, whenever the space is available for them to contend freely. However, certain constants are discernible: although the types of appropriation that look toward the "already-said" may seem to predominate, they tend to ossify the communal body; the approaches that tend to detach the "not-yet-said" from the text liberate the faith group from the repetition that could provoke a historical dislocation and a whole chain of unpleasant consequences.

For example, a "reiterative" reading of the royal "war" psalms, the Book of Judges, or even Exodus has led many Christians to "read" as well the events of the recent war between Israel and Egypt as modern replays of the traditional stories of the "passage through the Red Sea" in which the pharaoh was drowned. Worse, because the defeat of Israel's enemies is celebrated in the Bible as deriving uniquely from the grace and will of God, these persons have justified by analogy the Israeli right of conquest as divinely sanctioned.

On the Muslim side, certain qur'anic passages that refer to disagreements between the Prophet and the Jewish tribes of Medina have prompted (at least in the popular mind) interpretations that would justify the diaspora and condemn the Jewish people to dispersion, thus forgetting the good relations that have generally prevailed over the centuries between Muslim communities and Jewish minorities.

A critical analysis, or an "eschatological perspective," would on the contrary portray the biblical texts or stories as a discourse, in terms of ancient history and ideology, on the divine desire for radical justice that would place its absolute power at the service of the most vulnerable in order to endow them with its integrity and, therefore, the possibility to serve God freely outside the wicked constraints of the (pharaonic) law of the strongest.

If the founding message is really subversive against those in power, all those powers that are mocked by the only Sovereign with a right to the obedience of those liberated by calling them to be a special people, then it is the latter group of readings that is organically faithful to the original intent of the qur'anic or biblical discourse.

If, therefore, the structural analysis of traditional language with its re-readings or rearticulations is neither descriptive nor (even less) normative, it must pursue its investigation until it can distinguish, not between true and false (a fantasy from the exact sciences applied to the interpretation of meaning), but between coherent and incoherent.

There is a profound grammar—logical rules of the game—that governs the articulation between the whole of these readings, states of society or experience, and the nature of the text. Among approaches to the text, there is a considerable variety of techniques. We know for example the need for, and the limitations of, historical criticism, which is indispensable to a contextual reading but repressive when it takes on totalitarian pretensions. We are also familiar with the current tendency to stress how *everything* is significant in a text, advancing techniques of reading that insist on respecting the minutest distinction, to the point of respecting anomaly and reviving the pleasure of reading, but introducing to it the gratuitousness that frees one from the intellectual constraints that the sacred could have imparted.

All these approaches, and others to come—for it will be necessary to invent some for a community of Muslim and Christian researchers—have in common the ability to launch a renewed relationship with the text and its readings.

The community's critical examination of the use of these techniques, which it has itself produced or which it has borrowed from elsewhere, has a decisive import. Not only can it account for the structural reality of the hermeneutic continuity in the community's history, but it can also contribute at least modestly, to illuminating whatever coherence exists between the history of its readings and the specificity of its eschatological expectations. Here, analysis can serve and combine with the theological development, as long as it does not confuse the different levels of language but keeps to its proper purpose by giving to the theologian the objective elements of an appreciation of the eschatological "thrust" which calls the believing community into being.

Finally, then, analyses of the functions of the book as a book, articulated with the various "sound" approaches to the text which share the will to read "more," inform the rigor of examination without needlessly traumatizing those societies which are perpetually threatened by a fundamentalist or literalist reaction. Unverified exegeses, erudite or otherwise, conservative or liberal, can indeed function as dogmatics and injure the community by giving it the idea that it ought to make a value judgment about one reading or, worse, about the original message.

2

Receiving Scripture
in Community

The text of this second chapter is the result of five years of work by the Muslim-Christian Research Group in Rabat. It was presented and studied in its successive stages of development at the annual assemblies in Tunis (1979), Sénanque (1980), and Rabat (1981).

In preparing this text the group developed its own modus operandi. At each of its monthly meetings, there were fairly free discussions of a theme set in advance; the records of these discussions, as edited with everyone's agreement, are the only materials from which the final text was fashioned. This gives the final product a particular tone, which may be disappointing when compared with the richness of the participants' conversations and less erudite than it would have been if it had been constructed from individually edited contributions, but the group wished above all to seek and move forward together. The members considered one point to have impressed them as essential to their phenomenological description of the relationship between the believer and scripture: as Christians and Muslims, we realize together that we share many attitudes and reactions, without denying the radical difference in the status of the text in our respective traditions.

MODES OF TRANSMISSION OF SCRIPTURE

Touching on communal celebrations, education, and the mass media, our first point attempts to describe how scripture is circulated and transmitted within our communities and to note some of the questions raised by these processes. So great is the diversity among the situations observed that we have felt it necessary to present the Christian and Muslim experiences separately before offering some common conclusions.

Communal Celebrations

In the Christian community, the Sunday religious service, and other observances, where they are honored, are designed for the practicing members of the community, who attend freely. They touch a limited group of interested and motivated persons. Other celebrations attract a larger number of participants: the major festivals, Christmas and Easter especially, but also the "occasional" functions of baptism (whether of children or adults), confirmation, marriage, and burial. A great many persons attend out of conformity, under the pressure of peer groups, or because of a vague feeling of belonging to the church in spite of a certain indifference. It is clear that these different constituents, convinced believers and casual Christians, are not addressed in the same way.

The liturgy, which has its culmination in the eucharist, includes prayers (which are often sung) of repentance, praise, and intercession, and also readings of the Word: Old and New Testament. In the Old Testament, the largest share is for the Psalms and the prophets; the most commonly quoted passages are those that proclaim the coming of salvation, and can thus be interpreted symbolically as announcing the coming of the Messiah-Christ. In the New Testament, readings come regularly from the Epistles of Paul, and of Peter, John, and James, who proclaim the faith in Christ crucified and resurrected, in whom persons have passed from death to life, to which they must bear witness, and the Acts of the Apostles. But it is the gospel text that gives each Sunday its special tone and determines in part the other texts. The reading of the Gospels, spread over three liturgical years, is practically complete; those for each year recall the principal events in Jesus' life and his teaching.

In celebrating some special rituals, the church takes the opportunity offered by a larger attendance to assemble a certain number of texts in order to proclaim the essence of the gospel message. Thus, the baptismal order insists that Christ himself instituted baptism (Matt. 28:18–20). Baptized persons are invited to recall their own baptism, as well as the commitments then taken before God and the community (Mark 10:13–16); the idea of belonging to a new community is evoked (Ezek. 36:24–27 or Jer. 31:31–34). At marriages, the church announces the Word, blesses the union of the new partners and intercedes for them. There are reminders of the serious nature of the mutual commitment, the indissolubility of marriage, fidelity to one's spouse, support "for better or for worse" (Gen. 1:27f.; Prov. 31:10ff.; Eccles. 9:9; Matt. 19:4–6; Eph. 5:21–33; 1 Cor. 7:1–6; 1 Pet. 3:1–7). During burials, the officiant speaks principally to the living, recalling that Christ has overcome death (John 11:25f.; Rom. 6:9–11), that we have the hope of another life (John 14:1–6; 6:37–40; 1 Cor. 15:20–27; 1 Thess. 4:13f.), that we must keep ourselves ready to meet God (Isa. 40:6–8; Matt. 24:36–44; 25:1–13; Mark 13:32–35; 1 Thess. 5:4f.).

Within all these liturgical groupings, we must also note the importance of preaching, which represents an attempt at actualization centered on the proclaimed texts; in this way, the church mediates the reception of scriptural texts. Commentary is based on exegesis and theology; it involves a call on believers to recognize that God loves them personally, and an invitation to submit their lives to the requirements of the Word of God.

For many Christians today, these communal celebrations are the only occasions for confronting the texts of scripture and the teachings of the church. They thus occupy a privileged position, not only as the place where scripture is passed on, but also as the present locus of the transmission and celebration of faith in the person of Jesus who, in the Spirit, leads to the Father. The scriptures themselves describe the progressive discovery of salvation history and communal faith in adhering to the divine mystery.

Concerning Islam, our task is not so much to describe ritual practices in precise detail as to show which events in a Muslim's life act as factors in the permanence of the scripture as a text or, in other words, as vectors of transmission.

Ritual prayer is pure worship, not petition. It is obligatory only in congregation on Friday. At other times, it is an individual responsibility. Five times a day, practicing Muslims turn toward their God, put themselves in God's hands, and try to detach themselves for a moment from their earthly preoccupations. For praying to the Creator, the believer can draw on God's Word. Prayer is of utmost importance as a mode of permanence for scripture, or at least for part of scripture.

We can thus wonder which sort of verses the believer recites during the prayer. Obviously, the range of verses used is broader when one's knowledge of the Qur'ān is more developed, but it is nevertheless true that certain verses recur more often than others. Special mention should be made of the *Fātiḥa*. which the believer contemplates at least seventeen times in twenty-four hours. Next, surahs 112 (Oneness) and 114 (Humankind) seem to be the most frequently recited. In general, one turns to the Meccan surahs, which are found near the end of the book (93–114) and are also the shortest. But there is nothing exclusive about this, for persons often recite the famous Throne Verse (255) of the second surah and the moving invocation of the last verse of the same surah (286). We should also mention the Light Verse (24:35) and the passage that recalls the wonderful names of God (59:22–24). The themes of those surahs and verses, which the believer ponders, flow from the following wellsprings: glorification of the Creator and recollection of God's principal attributes (oneness, transcendence, omnipotence, but especially mercy and compassion, which are mentioned at the beginning of every surah), exhortation to accomplish one's religious and social obligations (an appeal for communal solidarity and justice), faith in the resurrection, and a future life in which persons will be treated according to the way they have lived.

The month of Ramadan is not just a month of fasting, but also a month of religious fervor: believers are more open to hearing scripture. A fair number of Muslims who normally neglect their prayers try for this period to be more scrupulous in their observation. Ramadan thus offers an opportunity for certain members of the community to renew contact with scripture through the prayers and to go more frequently to the mosque. The fast prepares the Muslim better to absorb the Word of God. During the Night of Power (27 Ramadan) the Muslim tries to relive the sending down of revelation; some believers stay in the mosques from the night-prayer (*'ishā*) until dawn, and the entire Qur'ān is recited in the framework of a collective prayer.

The pilgrimage (*hajj*) is a moment of utter availability for prayers and ceremonies. Besides, the faithful are very eager to say their prayers together. At this time, a particular fervor can be sensed, because of the numbers, the place, and the absolute equality among the believers who have come from every corner of the community. During the pilgrimage, the prayers are not exclusively worship, but include prayers of invocation and appeals for the intercession of the Prophet.

Funerals provide a special opportunity for people to recite and contemplate the Word, but particularly for believers to meditate on their own destiny: Muslims are sure that death is not the end of all life, but a necessary gateway to the life after resurrection. When death deprives them of someone dear, believers are deeply affected but not offended, for they accept the divine will and think of these verses:

Yours is the promise of a day which ye cannot postpone nor hasten by an hour [34:30].

Every soul shall taste of death, and We try you with evil and good for a testing; then unto Us you shall be returned [21:35].

The deeper their faith, the more will believers welcome death with a certain serenity and hope to be among those of whom the Qur'ān says:

O thou soul at peace, return unto thy Lord, well-pleased, well-pleasing, and enter among My servants; enter My paradise! [89:27–30].

Before the deceased is carried to the cemetery, there is a ceremonial reading from the Qur'ān, during which divine mercy is invoked; those present recite surah 36, which is addressed more to the living than the departed, given that it stresses the inevitability of resurrection and retribution. It is a veritable alarm bell to awaken backsliders (verses 51–83).

Education

Within the Christian community transmission of the faith is primarily a family responsibility, but it is also the duty of the community at large. That is why the churches organize catechism, according to a number of slightly varying forms that share a common objective. Catechism is based mainly on scripture. It seeks to present itself in a spiritual climate in which the

Word of God can facilitate the discovery of the person of Jesus and an entry into the divine mystery.

From an early age, children are welcomed into the church and introduced to the Christian message. In particular they are taught from the New Testament about the life of Jesus from his birth to his death, the gifts of the Spirit, the liturgical festivals (Christmas, Easter, Pentecost), Jesus's miracles (the Cana wedding, the healings, the man born blind, the centurion's servant, the feeding of the thousands, the miraculous catch of fish, Jesus walking on the water), the parables (the good Samaritan, the lost sheep, the prodigal son, the murderous laborers), the history of the first Christian communities, Paul's vocation, Stephen's martyrdom.

In the Old Testament, emphasis is given to the history of the covenant, with reference to those texts that are most accessible to children, such as those concerning the most important personalities and events in sacred history: Adam and Eve, Cain and Abel, Noah and the flood, the tower of Babel, Abraham and his sacrifice, Esau and Jacob, the stories of Joseph and Moses, Joshua and Samuel, Job and his dungheap. It is thus a collection of wonderful tales, often torn from their mythical or historical context, which continues to pervade the religious universe of many believers well beyond childhood.

But catechism should be joined to real life, to a spiritual experience, to a life in the Spirit. There should thus be a repeated effort to link these "stories" to situations familiar to children. This will be especially true when the catechism is addressed to adolescents preparing for their profession of faith or confirmation—that is, their entry into the community of "adult believers." We would choose themes from life, which could be illustrated with passages, often quite short, presented as responses to the questions that young persons ask or the aspirations they feel, such as sharing (John 2:1–12; 21:1–17), service (John 13:13–15; Mark 10:43–45), reconciliation (Luke 15:20–24), happiness (the Beatitudes), the role of the Spirit (John 14:16).

After confirmation, most Christians receive no more systematic teaching from the Word. But the churches offer a number of activities based on teaching and deepening the faith, designed to supplement Sunday sermons. These activities attract only a small number of believers, generally those who have a more regular and personal approach to the texts. Seasonal cycles of group Bible studies, which are sometimes organized ecumenically, are arranged under the leadership of a competent person: brief reading and practical study of a Gospel, or a selection of passages around a given theme. Because several readers are thus assembled to discover the meaning together, a number of different readings are heard. These readings question and stimulate one another. This live reading, in the contemporary context, allows the text to take on renewed meaning. Elsewhere, in seminars on "theological culture," Christians work under the guidance of theologians and exegetes to elaborate methods of approaching the texts and developing a variety of readings. A larger public is invited to lecture series (in Lent, etc.) as well as spiritual sessions or retreats.

In areas of a strict Reformed tradition, families conduct short Bible studies every day, often just before the main meal. At such times, households use prepared booklets of Bible readings and notes.

There are other vectors of religious tradition, such as the lives of saints and books of piety, which have sometimes acquired such importance that reading them could in certain cases take the place of reading the Scripture.

In Islam, piety (*taqwā*) in its fullest sense is a function of knowledge. The Qur'ān says: "Only those with knowledge fear God" (35:28). As other quotations could demonstrate, knowledge is not only indispensable to the believer individually, but it is so as well in consolidating the community of Muslims and in sustaining Islamic values. Hence the Prophet's insistence on the valuable role of education, as shown in this *hadith*: "To him for whom God has goodwill God attributes the gift of understanding. Knowledge is acquired only from learning." During his prophetic career Muhammad had offered the example of a teacher who would explain to his disciples the meaning of revelation and the teachings of Islam, and provide them with rules of conduct for every type of problem. Until the last century, this traditional teaching remained the only one with any validity in Muslim countries, so that a believer, whether educated or not, was immersed in a homogeneous cultural climate in which the different disciplines studied presented a web of complementarity and tended to a single system of religious and ethical values.

Religious instruction was articulated, and is still articulated today, around four axes: the Qur'ān, the Prophet's personality (*sīra*) and especially his sayings (*hadith*), human duties toward God (the five pillars), and Islamic morality. In the study of the Qur'ān, of which even non-Arabs learn long passages by heart, more attention is often given to memorization than to comprehension, for children normally start by learning the shortest surahs, and these are not necessarily the simplest (e.g., the eschatological verses). It is significant that these qur'anic passages are recited at length as a basis or support for the other three axes, so that the Word of God constitutes the essential element in the religious instruction dispensed by the schools.

Scripture continues to be disseminated beyond school age through optional courses at the mosques, Friday homilies, and public readings between the last two prayers of the day.

But insofar as the traditional cultural system ossified, religious instruction became more and more archaic. It was thus fatal for such a system to be brought under scrutiny after the great trials that the Muslim world suffered during its centuries of decadence, its ever-expanding contacts with the secular states of the West, and, especially, the constraints imposed upon it by a worldliness and a modernity of increasing influence. Traditional instruction was progressively marginalized because it had lost, in large measure, one of its major functions, which was the education of public servants at all levels. Its place in the economy was consequently diminished and it owes its survival to the loyalty of parents and the vigilance of religious and political authorities. In responding to the *salafiyyah* movement, governments have indeed undertaken to revitalize this teaching and adapt it to our times. Modern education (public and private) in various parts of the Islamic world has thus integrated religious disciplines into its curricula and tried to reinforce their effectiveness by placing them on the same level as profane subjects by designing adequate syllabi, publishing textbooks, setting examinations, and training officials. In the majority of cases, of course, the problem of the secular character of education has never been faced by the authorities. The old institutions—universities, traditional madrasahs, fraternities, zawiyahs—continue to thrive as always in certain sectors of the populace. Modern associations more in favor of radically transforming the spirit of this teaching have formed around the theme of the living reality of Islam. But can we say that all these efforts have been crowned with success?

Except for the fundamentalist currents that would transform Islam into an ideology of political combat, the new generations taken together are no longer motivated by this teaching, which has not produced the profound reforms needed. Its transformations have been purely external, for nothing has really changed in terms of content, method, or pedagogy: the historical is confused with the timeless, and the commentary with the text, so that the teaching continues to appear as a dogmatic entity.

Considered in its entirety, then, it is no longer able to establish a useful relationship between scripture and the daily life of the believer. Hence the elaboration of precepts and ideals tends toward apology and so turns away from painful reality to take refuge in a mythical past. We need to try other paths, as yet unblazed, to reestablish this relationship. Thanks to the boldness of a few thinkers, a few seekers, a new reading of the Qur'ān is still possible and desirable, and it may even be at the source of a genuine revolution in this teaching.

Beyond this description of education in our two communities, we observe together that it is *difficult to transmit to children a text conceived for an adult world*; it is impossible to say everything at once to children. Choices must be made, a progressive presentation must be designed. This could lead, more or less consciously, to an arbitrary selection of texts. Similarly, in order to interest adolescents in religion, one could be induced to choose the texts that they like.

We also observe that in each of our communities *religious education is generally provided during childhood but not adequately thereafter*, unless by the mass media. But cultural training continues and the critical mind is developed. In the training of many believers, therefore, *there is a misalignment between the cultural and the religious*, which may lead to the rejection of the religious insofar as it can no longer be justified. This rejection seems inevitable if a child's imagination has been filled with the marvelous alone. This childhood religious training leaves deep marks on the believer's imagination, which in turn is susceptible to perverse abuse. Zionism and apartheid, to mention only two examples, have made use of such elements in their development.

Finally, *we deeply regret*, and with a common accord, *that the Christian faith is not presented to Muslims, nor the Muslim faith to Christians*. To be sure, Islamic instruction has a place for biblical personalities from the Old and New Testaments (Jesus and Mary, in particular), but within the limits of an Islamic perspective; Christians do not find their bearings there. With a few rare exceptions, Christian teaching ignores the Muslim faith. When one faith is presented by others, there is often an element of caricature. Such teaching does not only fail to encourage intercommunal encounter; it actually risks perpetuating antagonism.

We recognize that the future of each community is linked to the transmission of its own faith. *A religious community cannot, therefore, be neutral in its teaching.* It is in fact profoundly implicated in this exercise. *But this ought not to push it to withdraw into itself and exclude others.* We think that progress in the quality of information and the respectful presentation of the other is both possible and necessary.

Mass Media

When one stops to think about it, it is surprising how important the mass media can be as a means of transmitting the Word of God.

When most Christians were illiterate, they were introduced to the personalities and scenes of the Bible through a great many visual representations: mosaics, frescos, icons, windows, tableaux, bas-reliefs, and even statues. Cathedral courtyards were well-suited to popular dramatizations. For example, the passion of Christ was presented each year in preparation for the Easter celebrations. And other biblical scenes were also performed as occasion warranted, thus nourishing a living popular tradition, which has continued into our own times.

The development of printing, which multiplied the chances of access to the text of scripture itself, had the side effect of diminishing the importance of figurative representations. Other texts were distributed along with the Bible, and today we know of a great many books on Bible study, commentaries, and spiritual guides, as well as a whole spectrum of reviews and journals of Christian inspiration, each of which transmits the texts of scripture in its own way.

With the extraordinary spread of music, especially since the appearance of phonograph records and then cassettes, the heritage of religious music has also orchestrated the Bible: Gregorian chant, passions, oratorios, requiems, Negro spirituals, Christmas carols, and the like. Photographs and slides bring a visual contribution to catechetic instruction. Cinema also reaches a very large public: such widely distributed films as *The Ten Commandments* have helped to give Moses a face, with all the ambiguities that this entails. Pasolini's *Gospel according to St. Matthew* and Zefirelli's *Jesus of Nazareth* are today setting a certain image of Jesus and his disciples in the same way as Leonardo's *Last Supper* or Rembrandt's *The Road to Emmaus* did for their own era.

Television allows viewers to share in certain important religious ceremonies or events (royal marriages, the funerals of heads of state or popes); it also makes possible the regular broadcasting of the Sunday liturgical celebration. Everywhere radio transmits religious music, ceremonies, and the like, and, in certain countries, a daily reading of a passage from the Word of God. It broadcasts in all directions, with no respect for religious frontiers; it can feed the faith of believers and foster an awareness of other scriptures, but it can also be the agent of an indiscreet proselytism.

Without wishing to strike a balance, we may observe that in Christianity *during every era*, according to varying modes, *the mass media have been proclaimers of the Word of God*; they have supported the memory and the faith of believers. They have also been able to impart a desire for a greater familiarity with the actual text of the scriptures. But every representation is ambiguous, especially perhaps when it is figurative; let us cite the example of the "fruit" in the Genesis story, which it would have been difficult to represent in the abstract. Custom has taken to showing it as an apple and many believers are persuaded that the apple is part of the text. *All representations and broadcasts through the centuries have been occasions to "reduce," or even deform, the message of the scriptures*; it is important to keep this in mind. *But they have also rendered it possible to bring the scriptures near the believers and make them real.*

In most Muslim countries, Islam is the state religion. The mass media (radio, television, and a large portion of the press) are controlled by the state. It is therefore quite natural that these means should be used, among others, for transmitting scripture. The case of Morocco is typical in this regard. Both radio and television stations begin and end their broadcasts with qur'anic psalmody. Programs are interrupted to send out the muezzin's call at the hours of ritual prayer, and the Friday prayer is broadcast in its entirety over the official airwaves. The same applies to religious ceremonies at festivals. During the winter of 1981–82, the mass media devoted extensive coverage to the rogatory prayers for rain. If to all this we add the courses of religious instruction, sermons, relaying of the Meccan pilgrimage, and so forth, we can say that, at least at a quantitative level, the information media play an important role in the transmission of scripture. They remind the faithful of the requirements of the faith and they tend to sustain the permanence of both Qur'ān and Sunnah.

It remains to be seen whether administering heavy doses of these often archaic and repetitive programs between much lighter fare (songs, films, sports) does not lead to the banalization of the Word of God by making it just another element in the endless murmur of official broadcasts. There would seem to be a saturation point beyond which we risk provoking obstruction and counterproductive effects.

As for the media in non-Muslim countries, these often give Islam a fragmentary and partisan image that is sometimes a caricature. The most striking example of this is the presentation of jihad, usually taken as holy war and sometimes even as a war to exterminate non-Muslims. The scripture is not judged on its own terms—that is, according to the principles and ideas that it advocates. Rather, it is judged according to the situation and behavior of contemporary Muslims. We note that Western radio, press, and television are often satisfied with an approximation, confusing Arabs with Muslims, or what is essentially Islamic with what is only superstition.

Films and plays (whether televized or not) mostly present historical scenes of an edifying character: there is an appeal to scripture or even more to the *sīra* (the life of the Prophet and his companions), all in a grandiloquent style that strikes the imagination. Televised films sometimes tell stories of the prophets based on qur'anic tradition. These emissions have the great advantage of relating, in a simple and even attractive way, episodes from sacred history that the greater public has not heard or may have forgotten. But we must emphasize that the person of Muhammad is never portrayed by an actor (consider the film *The Message*).

In spite of a difference in the status of images, this survey of the mass media reveals that the two communities have much in common. But *we observe an important cleavage between countries with an official religion, whether Christian or Muslim, and secular states.* In the former, the mass media, especially television, amply diffuse religious information and a respect for religion, so many scriptural passages are transmitted. In the others, religious information becomes utterly marginal, sometimes even caricatural, and the text of the scriptures is very rarely passed on.

In concluding this presentation of the modes of transmitting scripture, we could wonder whether the same process does not govern the transmission of the message in every faith community. We can only affirm that the *institutions established for the transmission of scripture are often inadequate,* and that the message is not always passed on in its entirety, or it is received in an inexact or deformed manner.

However, the faith communities continue to live on the message of the scripture, which does not lose its flavor. We could wonder, then, where *the focuses of the revivification of this message* are today. In the quest for new types of human relations in the political, social, and cultural fields, we may perhaps find those vital forces that must facilitate the development of a renewed meaning of the revelations within the religious communities. As well, the experience of spiritual individuals brings new life to the message of the revelation.

READINGS OF SCRIPTURE

As Christians and Muslims, we note together that the reading of the Bible and the Qur'ān has assumed certain modalities according to historical periods and cultural regions. Each community of believers has, according to its own sensitivities, favored one aspect or another of the text to the detriment of other aspects, which it has more or less left in the shadows.

But, thanks to the many meetings of individuals and communities that the modern world allows, the relative character of these readings rooted in particular traditions is becoming more apparent, as is the richness of readings from other milieux.

Factors That Influence the Reading of Scripture

These factors may be communal or individual.

At the communal level we must first note the factor of *distance in relation to the letter*. Analysis shows that contact with the text is not as direct as it may seem to be in the two traditions. In prayer and the events of life, for Muslims as for Christians, rites derived from the text occupy a large place, but the text as such is not really known. Priority is given to the concern for communion around a message. Before understanding and developing the meaning, the believer wants to adhere, to find someone or something in which to trust. For many Muslims in non-Arabic countries, unfamiliarity with Arabic prevents direct contact with the text. The use of language different from ordinary speech has not made it easy for Christians to read the text directly.

Distance from the letter is compounded by *socio-cultural distance*. The centuries since the appearance of our scriptures have been laden with history; new cultural references have arisen while others have faded away. Inexorably, a cultural gap is opening as time goes on, and it is becoming more acute with urbanization and industrialization. This makes it even more difficult to approach the text, especially when readers are unaware of the cultural gap.

There is also a *distance from the meaning*. Whether we refer to the text of the Qur'ān or to biblical texts, verses or entire passages can be memorized without having access to the meaning of the whole text. Persons also know the story of Adam, the flood, of Joseph or Moses, partly through the popular preaching that twists or even falsifies the meaning. Beliefs are often derived more from earlier superstitions than from a reading of the actual texts. Christians know the parables or the life of Jesus through a moralizing package that has become denser with the passing centuries and masks the forceful character of the text.

Finally, the faith community does not easily adapt its life to the appeals of revelation, so it accepts and justifies practices that are contrary to the spirit of scripture. It therefore finds a new difficulty in understanding the meaning of the text and thus reinforces the distances already established with a *practical distance*.

To these communal factors must be added an important individual coefficient that marks, just as in human relations, the relationship of the Word of God defined by the scriptural message. Every believer who adheres to this word perceives that this adherence of heart and soul cannot always be explained, that its fulfillment lies partly beyond the rational and is bound to the believer's own aspirations and training. This personal factor explains the great diversity of religious sensitivity and behavior, and the variety in relationship to the text among the members of the same community.

Within the community, then, scholars, exegetes, or theologians, drawing on a vast religious background and a rich conceptual framework, can penetrate and analyze specific aspects of the text. This confers on them the authority, and indeed the power, to read and interpret the text, and so to enrich theological tradition.

Spiritual persons who feed on the Word of God are capable of penetrating the text in their own way, even without any training in religious sciences. To the extent that the heart is available to God's call and in the measure that life is patterned according to this call, spiritual persons have an authenticity that affords them access to the depths of the divine message before many others. The witness of such a person's life and, sometimes, writings contributes to the enrichment of the spiritual tradition, fulfilling a recall function that is of great importance to the believing collectivity (Benedict of Nursia, Abu Madyan of Tlemcen, Ibn Abbad of Ronda, Francis of Assisi, Ibn Arabi, Theresa of Avila, Abd al-Qadir al-Jilani, and many more).

Tendencies Inherent in a Communal Reading

The quest for coherence and the affirmation of orthodoxy are the major tendencies linked to a communal reading.

QUEST FOR COHERENCE

For each community, to read is to seek coherence. But there is a risk of raising this relative coherence to the absolute when secondary issues are being considered. We have noticed that each community tends to settle into a certitude that points to a justification of acquired habits and thereby to establish itself as a sort of rival to other groups. Every community tends to maintain its own reading, especially in the face of the challenges posed by historical circumstances or certain currents of thought (modernism, liberalism, materialism) or even by religious experiences different from its own. The danger is a desire to universalize one reading or another as the only one in conformity with the truth of the text.

As a certain systemization is necessary to maintain a coherence in thought, just like a certain order sustains social cohesion, there have been numerous attempts in history to systemize the readings of the texts. In both Christianity and Islam, the confrontation of believers' faith with various cultures and events has led from the founding texts to theological elaboration expressed in terms of schools of thought and collective positions that have at times even rent the community asunder and brought into question the received orthodoxy. Examples are well-known in both traditions.

We should also remember that fundamentalist and integrist readings, often colored by politics, have been common over the centuries in each community.

The Qur'ān and the Bible are both open to restrictive readings, which insist on what concerns the community's internal affairs, and to broader readings, which situate the community in relation to others.

Today, two elements favor a more open, less dogmatic, reading of the texts. In the first place, there are encounters with other types of culture or sensitivity. In the second, there is the recognition of a plurality of readings of religious texts, and of their oral and fragmentary character, which does not permit them to be shut into an exclusive reading. The texts are bearers of a plural truth. Scripture is an abundance, not a unique system.

AFFIRMATION OF ORTHODOXY

The definition of orthodoxy at any given time poses some complex problems; it cannot be the work of the community as a whole. It is elaborated through the normative efforts of specialists working on the foundation texts. But this labor is undertaken in response to appeals and contributions, sometimes contradictory, coming from the community of believers who are confronted with various problems in their spatio-temporal context.

Within every community there is a constant, complex tension among the authorities who appropriate the text on various grounds.

On the political level, religion is an arena for historical struggles. In times of tension, the text is inflexible and in times of dialogue there is more openness. Thus, interpretations of the idea of jihad pass, according to circumstances and personalities, from an external war against the enemy to an internal moral struggle. Thus, too, the question of the legitimacy of violence against others, which was rejected by Christianity before Constantine, has since been generally accepted, even to the point of sanctioning a "just war."

On the theological level each tendency strives to render exclusive the interpretation of the text that reflects its own point of view. It is thus with questions of fatalism, free will, or predestination in the two traditions. Whenever a given generation has agreed on a synthesis that seemed perfect and sufficient—ash'arism or Thomism—rereading of the text has been blocked for some time. Similar situations arise whenever a community has reached the limits of ideological appropriation, as when Jesus was reduced to the role of a wise master in the eighteenth century, religious guide in the nineteenth, or liberator or guru in the twentieth. Such situations also occur in Islam, as when the caliphates of Abu Bakr and Umar are considered to be the "golden age" of authentic democracy and Islamic socialism.

On the spiritual level, reading swings between a closed position, an impermeability to anything disturbing, and an openness that spiritual persons themselves have invited by their manner of rereading the text. Their reading illumines and completes the sayings of the prophets, which thus become new for those who are listening.

These diverse tensions give rise to contradictory attitudes all claiming inspiration from the same text. In fact, each instance tends to appropriate the text according to its own interests and aspirations. It is remarkable that in every case the mechanism of appropriation tends to make the text its own to the exclusion of all others. In this way, orthodoxy and heterodoxy are not defined so much by what they maintain but by what they reject. Indeed, a partial interpretation of the meaning cannot claim to appropriate the whole text without becoming totalitarian; that is, in its partiality excluding the other and the difference between them.

Now, *this tendency to appropriation/exclusion is rejected by the biblical or qur'anic text*, which, if it is considered in its entirety, forbids the rejection of the other that we so readily practice. The denial of the other leads inexorably to a resistance to change, to a denial of an embarrassing revelation, to a refusal to be challenged by the text. And the danger that lurks is the temptation for humans to supplant God's authority with their own claims and make believe that their will and desires are the translation of the sense of the scripture. Such a legitimation of human acts leads to a partial and stunted reading of the meaning of scripture.

Durability of Scripture

But scripture endures and our chances for a better reading are based on scripture itself to the extent that it resists every manipulation and recovery. So it stimulates and renews the believers' faith even as it sustains new believers.

A perpetual rereading is the work of every living community. History has shown that these rereadings, which have developed around the text to produce new meanings within the continuing tradition, have been challenged and stimulated by the research of scholars, the concerns of those who thirst after righteousness and the intuitions of mystics.

Certainly, the application of recent scientific methods to the reading of the text is a difficult enterprise, which overturns inherited attitudes. But this rereading is enriching for the faith communities. It enhances the essence of the faith and it can help distinguish the social and historical from the transcendent. Those who thirst for justice also challenge and stimulate the traditions, whereas the dominant classes, who wish to preserve their privileges, favor any reading that does not question the established order. Poverty, an attitude of dependency and need, invokes divine justice against human injustice; among the oppressed this elicits an openness of heart for a renewed reading. Finally, in each community there are also many persons who, entranced by the absolute, have enriched the study of the text by their ardent search for truth and their sense of contemplation, developing a reading that is more spiritual than others and more detached from contingencies.

So, although revelation is historically dated, the fulness of its meaning must be continuously sought and explored. Believers are called to a continuous effort to draw ever nearer to the sense of the scripture and to pattern their life on it. The more that believers pattern their life on the scripture, the more its meaning will be clear to them, and the mode of understanding the scripture will transform their mode of being so that their life will change.

BY ACCEPTING SCRIPTURE, BELIEVERS LIVE "DIFFERENTLY"

Whatever may be the imperfections of Christian and Muslim "civilization" and the deficiencies of the modes of transmitting the scripture in either tradition—it is banal indeed to note how little difference there is between the adherents of any given religious message and those who have no explicit affiliation to any faith group—the believers of goodwill (to speak only of them) are nevertheless conditioned by the scripture in their deepest perceptions. We therefore find it impossible to describe "objectively" the reality of the spiritual and religious life of believers today without referring to the scriptural anthropology that underlies their behavior and acts as a norm by which to measure religious experience. Therein lies the kernel of this third section: by accepting the scripture, believers discover God's calling as well as their own imperfection and greatness; they become aware of the gap between the call of the scripture and their own comportment, and they feed their hope. We are certainly aware that the anthropology outlined here would need a fuller analysis for each idea raised.

Believers Discover God's Call and Their Own Imperfection and Greatness

THE SCRIPTURE FORMULATES THE CALLINGS TO WHICH INDIVIDUALS ARE PERMANENTLY INVITED AND THE OBLIGATIONS TO WHICH THEY ARE SUBJECTED AS AN AFFIRMATION OF GOD'S UNIVERSAL LORDSHIP

In this regard, we can detect *thematic similarities* in the two traditions: the requirements of faith, justice, forgiveness, love, "commanding goodwill," all derive from a comparable inspiration and form the axes of those calls that the believer, Christian or Muslim, discerns in the scripture. There are also evident similarities in the manner in which these themes are announced: whether we think of Jesus or Muhammad, the prophetic function is one of recalling the requirements of divine justice that human beings have rejected.

Two essential themes seem to demonstrate a genuine convergence between the Bible and the Qur'ān: obedience to God, and God's mercy. In the New Testament, a person's duty, the only means of attaining the fulness to which persons are called, is obedience to God; this obedience one can know and practice through the mediation of Jesus. In Islam, submission to God is the supreme way, humanity's reason to be as perceived through the Qur'ān and the *sīra* (life of the Prophet). Jesus proclaims the forgiveness of sins, and God is merciful in Islam.

But there are also differences of emphasis that are more than nuances. A careful examination will indeed show that Christian anthropology generally leads to a dialectical understanding of the link between God and humans: divine love comes first, God saves, God redeems, persons who in this love discover their sin and who, through this prevenient forgiveness, experience the revelation of the infinite love that conveys it. Islamic anthropology develops a conception of this link that is immediate and calm: "The good person is one who believes in God" and who acts justly.

The scripture offers a model that can enlighten each era. Faced with the magnitude of our current problems, believers are led to reread their scriptures with a special seriousness. Observing that, from personal life to international affairs, conflicts arise because justice is often mocked and every individual finds it difficult to recognize for others not just their due but even their right to exist, each believer turns to scripture in the hope of finding the true meaning of justice. The same is true with regard to the violence that so assaults our times (personal, social, economic, political, ideological violence, and abuses of power). To meet these challenges—or any others—of the contemporary world, believers are somehow summoned to renew their reading of scripture.

THE SCRIPTURE: AN EXPLANATION OF HUMANITY AND HUMAN DESTINY

The scripture is not limited to formulating the obligations and aspirations to which humanity is permanently subjected or invited—which comprise the ideal background for any religious life—but is also an explanation of humanity and human destiny.

The Christian and Muslim traditions each contain an anthropology, a comparative study of which allows us to perceive a common dynamic: human nature is divided between misery and greatness. Adam the prototype expresses this duality very well: the angels bow before him, but he is the sinner expelled from paradise. Thus, the human being is a fragile and contingent creature who, once created, manifests versatility, violence, and ingratitude, as we can learn from several accounts: Cain and Abel, the flood, the story of Joseph, and so on. The human being is weak and fallible.

But our greatness is no less real. The Spirit of God is infused in human persons, causing them to share in some of the divine attributes: intelligence, free will, speech. The human is created to serve God in terms of a finality that is both earthly (the human is the *khalīfa* of God in creation, a genuine lieu-tenant, manager of the world and servant of God) and heavenly (transcending what is here below and, called to resurrection, becoming worthy to see God). Created by God and destined to return to God, the human being is put to the test, between this beginning and this end.

Human beings, living in history, have felt divided, receiving the invitation of scripture to consider themselves as neither monsters nor angels, but to recognize their need for resurrection and an escape from their imperfection.

The Gap between the Callings of Scripture and the Behavior of Believers, in the Two Traditions

When we consider the scriptural requirements and the life of those who claim allegiance to them, we observe a wide gap which seems to be a constant in the history of our two communities. Believers who are aware of this gap necessarily live in a state of tension: their personal or communal situation appears to be a long way from the ideal presented by the scriptures. The history of our communities, which repeats this gap in a variety of forms, also relates the efforts of believers to reduce it.

The scriptures bear witness to this gap. Human beings created "in the image of God" (Gen. 1:27; *hadith*), God's vicars on earth, responsible for their actions, are the ones who have offended against the divine precepts:

The heart of a human person is evil from youth upwards [Gen. 8:21].

I do not understand what I do; what I do is not what I want to do, but what I detest [Rom. 7:15].

The soul incites to evil, unless my Lord has mercy [Eccles. 12:53].

Successive prophets have denounced these deviations, these infidelities, this dereliction of duty:

Like Adam, they have broken my covenant [Hos. 6:7].

You did not recognize God's moment when it came [Luke 19:44].

If they see a sign, they do not believe in it. If they see the path of righteousness, they do not take it as their way. If they see the path of error, they take it as their way. They act in this manner because they treat our signs as falsehood and because they do not care [Eccles. 7:146].

A consideration of contemporary social organization and human behavior allows us to recognize this gap at several levels. At the international level there are flagrant inequalities between rich and poor nations of the same faith (such as North and South America or Arab oil states and their resource-poor neighbors); believers are accomplices to the arms trade; situations like apartheid are sometimes justified in the name of the scriptures; societies condone games of chance, drug abuse, and usurious practices in places where they are strictly forbidden; ideas of fraternity, solidarity, tolerance, respect of human dignity are ridiculed daily, in the very countries that claim to follow Christian or Muslim traditions. This gap, which crosses all social life, is also to be found in the hearts of believers.

But the scriptures call us to narrow this gap. Even as we are aware of it, we know that an authentic commmunal religious praxis will lead to a narrowing of the gap. Faithfulness to scripture and its requirements is made manifest by worship, meditation on the Word, and witness, which gradually introduce the believer to a new vision of the world and a desire to change it in conformity with prophetic exhortations. It is at times like these that faithfulness shows itself less in a congealed ritual observance than in a quest for and discovery of the new meanings that such practices can assume today. The gaps experienced by each generation must give rise to new responses, the signs of a renewed faithfulness.

But the gap remains. Even if the sense of the law is renewed for believers today, even if their behavior changes accordingly, the gap, in which believers existentially appear to their own eyes, remains. *The awareness of this gap seems to us therefore to be an essential element of the believers' situation.*

By Accepting Scripture, Believers Feed Their Hope

Scripture, which gathers believers within a framework of attitudes and practices, is thus a source of renewals or transformations, of the heart of each believer as well as the actions of the community. In this way, the almohad, salafi, or reformist readings have been the wellsprings of new collective life. The scripture here not only guides and directs, but it also produces a change in the individual and collective being of believers.

The Word of God disturbs, upsets, interrogates. It forces radical revisions. It dynamizes the whole of existence as one can observe, for example, in the three degrees of life that Islam offers. The first, *islām*, represents an external adherence to Islam, sometimes colored by formalism and often limited to a simple utterance of the *shahāda*. This is a token of belonging to the community. *Imām*, which is more enlightened and involves the adherence of the heart and mind, stimulates personal exertion by which believers go beyond the first degree even as they achieve it. *Iḥsān* carries the conviction of living in the sight of God and following God's guidance: the believer goes beyond the first two states and may accede to the contemplative vision.

Regular study of scripture allows Christians who are open to the Spirit to discover the greatness of their calling and the power of the resurrection at work in the world. They know in whom they have trusted and they grow to adulthood in this faith, which culminates in the vision of God. Regular study of scripture invites each believer to pass from a banal sociological practice marked by religious gestures to a more personal practice marked especially by service to others, and finally to a desire for intimacy with God through prayer and a practice marked by the spirit of the "Beatitudes."

As we have already indicated, believers, whether Muslim or Christian, who seek to deepen faith in a more personal relationship to scripture and try, through openness to God and the practice of God's Word, to narrow the gap that remains between God's call and their own conduct, will observe paradoxically how the gap persists—and even seems to widen—between practical faithfulness and the infinite import of this Word.

Awareness of the gap could discourage believers, but it could also incite them to renew their trust in God, thanks to the promises to which the scriptures bear witness. This awareness drives believers to bear witness of the hope that is in them, to make the task of recall their own. This witness is the link by which the believer can gain access to a personal relationship with the text, which thus becomes a personal relationship with the God who calls.

By living from scripture, witnesses are led to contest certain practices within their community and that can in turn induce them to run the risk of being condemned by the established authorities.

In their life and spiritual quest, believers refine judgments of their own actions and radicalize these acts in the measure of personal faith. The religious act is thus always both a faithfulness to a tradition, a re-statement, and a rupture, a novelty in relation to a personal history. The act of believing is a decision that finds real meaning based on a tradition and a drawing away from it with a view to a re-creation.

3

The Scriptures of One Community as Seen through the Faith of the Other

The text of this third part was elaborated during a period of five years by the Tunis group, based first of all on communications on the various points presented by several of its members. These presentations were discussed by the group, then reworked as a synthesis of the labors of the whole group. That report, which was particularly voluminous in its historical consideration of thirteen centuries of Christian attitudes towards the Qur'ān, was condensed and then presented to the general meeting of Tunis-Korbous (September 1982). After a thorough discussion, it was amended to take account of the observations offered during this gathering.

PRELIMINARY REMARKS

Thus far we have tried to find an approach common to Christians and Muslims for analyzing the phenomenon of scripture and describing its reception by believers personally and in community. We think that we should go further and try to take account of our partner's scripture in our own vision of faith. The Christian should be able to situate the Qur'ān in the Christian perspective of revelation, and the Muslim ought to be able to set the Bible in the Muslim understanding of revelation.

There is no lack of warning against such an undertaking these days, from Muslims and Christians: history has shown that such "theological" approaches always degenerate into apologetic and polemic, which can only harm our mutual understanding; let us therefore limit our encounter and approach to the regular relations of life and common endeavor. To try to go further could lead to unwarranted presumptions about the mystery of revelation, of the divine plan in communicating the Word of God to humanity. Would this not produce an "indiscreet theology" or even lapse into a simple mental game?

We do not think so, for reasons that we derive both from our experience of Christian-Muslim encounter and from the requirements of our faith.

Our experience has shown us how genuine encounter between Christians and Muslims can be compromised by the presuppositions and prejudices articulated by our respective traditions and rooted in our thought-forms. Sometimes they are expressed spontaneously, naively. When they are not voiced, they pervade, whether consciously or not, many attitudes of rejection or mistrust. However much goodwill we may each have, how can a Christian who thinks that the Qur'ān is only the work of a man who was more or less informed, or even—there are those who say so—the work of the "Evil One," share deeply in the life of his Muslim partner? Or how can Christians hear the call to prayer, the chanting of the Qur'ān on the radio or television, or read the Qur'ān and find therein a stimulating interrogation of their own faith? Where could Muslims find the message of Jesus, this "Gospel" to which the Qur'ān refers, if they are persuaded that the text of the Bible, and especially of the canonical Gospels, is in no way authentic? How could they avoid thinking, in the depths of their heart, that their best Christian friend is on the road to perdition? Far too often, instinctive and clumsy reactions cut short the best discussions or at least prevent them from bearing their full harvest.

But this view of faith about the scripture of the other is also, perhaps primarily, an impulse to seek the truth. We all believe that the light that God gives us in revelation should illumine our vision of the world and guide our action. Our encounter with believers from another religion has made us feel that they have an authentic faith and religious experience. This faith and experience have their source and reference point in scripture considered to be the Word of God. How could we accept on either side that this vital reference was only an illusion?

Here we come to the central problem. Our scriptures each present themselves as a global, universal, recapitulative message and the "theologies" that issue from them have not neglected to accentuate further this absolute, exclusive character. We can doubtless remark a certain inequality on this point between the Bible and the Qur'ān: the Bible could not mention the Qur'ān, which came six centuries after the biblical text was established, whereas the Qur'ān refers in its text to the Torah and the Gospel. But the problem is basically the same: How can I recognize a divine origin for the sacred text that inspires, concretely, the life of my partner? How can I reconcile the fulness that my scripture brings to me with the authenticity of the other's scripture? The testimonies of believers engaged in this adventure of deep encounter with the believers of another faith and the questions they ask themselves are sufficient proof of the validity and the urgency of this quest.

Of course, we could be content with an "existential" attitude: I find the fulness of inspiration for my life in my scripture, and I observe that my partner does the same in his or hers. How can these two experiences, equally understood as authentic, be reconciled? Only God knows. We can only respect the mystery and live, each in our own context, the Word we have received.

This attitude seems eminently respectable to us. We adopt as our own the respect for God's mystery and revelation to which it testifies. But we think that the intelligence of faith can suggest other ways of thought that could account for a certain *coherence* between the teachings of our scriptures and our experience of the faith of our partners. Indeed, we believe that progress in theological research in our two religions allows us to consider several factors that could, in part, pose the problem in new terms.

First, if believers find the fulness of their religious yearning in their own scripture, can they conclude thereby that this scripture is the exhaustive expression of the Word of God, that it reveals everything that God can say to human beings about God's mystery? In the logic of our previous affirmation, according to which the revelation of God's Word is always "indirect" because it is always transmitted in human language, we do not think so. No human speech, even as an expression of God's own Word, can be coextensive with this Word and express it completely. There is therefore room, in principle, for an articulation of God's Word besides the one to which our own scripture bears witness.

Moreover, even if the text of our scriptures is "closed," their "reading" or meaning for us is not closed as long as we live, as long as the world continues. Each "reading" of the book has been marked by the experience of its times. How could this not be so again today?

To the extent that the other's vision of scripture has been influenced in the past by a climate of confrontation between two empires, new relationships that are growing between us encourage the development of a substantially new meaning. Theology is not exempt from the fundamental principle according to which every reading (or interpretation) — like every oral or written document — is largely conditioned by the reader's, and the speaker's, personal situation, and by its living context (space, time). Believers see in the evolution of the world a call from God to reread their scripture in order to draw from its inexhaustible richness a response to the questions of today's human beings. Our research would be a contribution to a sense of scripture for our times.

But it is not only the sense of our scriptures, the sense of their very text, which needs to be renewed. Also, and perhaps especially, the "theological" categories that have been derived from our scriptures must be subjected to critical reflection. It is a well-known fact that the theology of revelation was elaborated, in Christianity and in Islam, from the sole phenomenon of revelation, in which our respective faiths have their origin. Afterward this theory was applied to the other phenomenon without considering its own peculiarities. The Christian theologian thus unilaterally applies certain recent theories of biblical inspiration to the Qur'ān — which resists. And the Muslim theologian applies the rules of literal transmission of the Qur'ān to the Bible, to the Gospels—which do not resist! We must therefore show a certain boldness and question afresh some well-established categories, categories established at a time when each side was wrapped up in its own truth and ignorant of the other. Today we believe that we must take account of the phenomenon of revelation wherever it occurs.

It goes without saying that the Christian view of the Qur'ān, however open it may be, cannot fully match the Muslim point of view, which is properly part of the Muslim faith. The same is true for the Muslim view of the Bible. We have insisted on respecting this fundamental difference. But our discussions have helped us to understand better our different approaches to scripture and to bring them together as nearly as possible.

The reflections that follow are the result of a genuine common effort between Christians and Muslims. They have been discussed and adopted in common meetings. But the subject they treat can be naturally divided into two parts, which we shall consider separately: a tentative new approach to the Qur'ān through Christian faith and a similar attempt by Muslim faith to approach the Bible (mainly the New Testament).

TOWARD A CHRISTIAN PERCEPTION OF THE QUR'ĀN

Our opening inquiry on this theme began with the *testimonies* of Christians in our group, deeply involved in encounter with Muslim believers. These questions that they ask themselves and that they ask theologians about the Qur'ān were the point of departure for our quest.

According to the natural methods of theology, we examined *our scripture, the Bible,* to find therein the initial orientation of our reflection. As there was obviously no question of finding references to the Qur'ān itself, our study of the Bible, Old and New Testament, focused on a more general query: To what extent can this scripture open the door to a recognition of an expression of God's Word to humanity that differs from its own? Next, it seemed useful—and even necessary—to look critically at the principal sources of the Christian *tradition* that derived from the Bible, from the origins of Christianity to our own day, that of the fathers of the church and that of the theologians, including the work of contemporary theologians and recent statements about Islam by the official representatives of the church. Christians were aware of the Qur'ān in the first century of its appearance (7th century). But we have preferred to go beyond the study of Christian attitudes to the Qur'ān, which are in any case overwhelmingly negative. Without neglecting this aspect, we have expanded the scope of our inquiry to seek, as in the case of the Bible, the possibility of openness toward other revelations. This applies of course to the six centuries that preceded the Qur'ān's appearance as well as to the subsequent period.

We could, then, present a few guidelines, some more traditional and others more novel, for a *contemporary Christian perception* of the Qur'ān.[1]

Questions Asked of Contemporary Christians

We shall not consider the prejudices—or illusions—still so widely circulated and often so ridiculous within a self-absorbed Christian world, nor even the impressions of a superficial reader of the Qur'ān who has established no contacts with persons who live by it. The testimonies we are about to cite are those of Christians, generally Westerners, who have entered into profound and friendly contact with Muslims, whether in an Islamic country or among migrants in Europe who are anxious to live there and remain faithful to their faith and its requirements.

These Christians were seldom prepared in any adequate way for their encounter and some were imbued with prejudices against the Islamic religion or even against any religious dimension treated as an alibi or refuge, but they discovered that the Qur'ān and the religious behavior it inspires were wellsprings of life, explanations for numerous practices, instinctive reactions or unconscious judgments. They therefore began to read the Qur'ān attentively, almost always in translation, and they were at one and the same time attracted by certain texts that resonated with religious experience and repelled by others concerning very human problems with no apparent religious value. This double experience (of a shared life and reading the Qur'ān) evoked a variety of reactions, which we can classify as follows:

1. The realization of how phenomenally ignorant the Christian world as a whole is about the Qur'ān, Islam, and Arab-Muslim culture, as though there were only two groups of persons in the world, Christians and unbelievers, completely overlooking non-Christian believers. "We have been deceived" by being taught, even at advanced levels, that Western culture was the universal culture, and it was likewise in terms of faith, when our Christian awareness was formed as though Islam did not exist.

2. The discovery of how "present" the Qur'ān is in the life of Muslims. It is rarely known in its entirety, but often memorized in snatches of verses that spring to mind in the myriad circumstances of life. Persons frequently refer to it: "It is in the Qur'ān . . . ," even if it is not really there, because they are aware that the Qur'ān is the source of all good conduct. But with this discovery there often comes an astonishment due to the apparently "mechanistic" understanding of revelation as the "descent" of a book that is ready-made, without the intervention of any human factor, and the consequent respect for the "book" and its letter, which is certainly edifying, could seem tantamount to idolatry of the text. Christians are also struck by the political and especially the apologetical exploitation of the Qur'ān manifested by representatives of certain tendencies, be they Islamic fundamentalists or the partisans of a scientific sublimation ("all modern sciences are found in the Qur'ān").

3. The discovery of the richness of the Qur'ān, not only on the esthetic or cultural plane, but as a book for Muslims, and for Christians too: "The

gospel is not my private treasure and I have a share in the Qur'ān." We are sensitive to the presence of God that imbues the Qur'ān, especially the notions of oneness, transcendence, and mercy, in the ethical requirements, the conception of life and death, the place of Jesus and Mary, with texts that have a gospel ring to them. Some reach the point of actually praying with the Qur'ān, for their own spiritual nurture and in union with their Muslim friends. But others, and even some from the first groups, are disturbed by other passages of the Qur'ān, which deal with questions of apparently little religious content: calls to "holy war," the law of talion (even if it provides for pardon), the urge for power, to say nothing of the numerous details concerning the organization of the community or the personal privileges of the Prophet. Where is the Word of God in all that? Compared to the gospel, the Qur'ān seems to be a return to the Old Testament.

4. More precisely, Christians can happily recognize in the Qur'ān the names of persons familiar to their own faith: Abraham, Moses, Zechariah, John the Baptist, Mary, Jesus. . . . But they balk at texts that seem to deny the Christian mysteries of the Trinity, the incarnation and divinity of Jesus, the cross and redemption, because they do not recognize fully the dogmas of their faith in the qur'anic formulations. But they also think that the dogmatic explanations of these mysteries elaborated by the councils and theologians in relation to particular historical circumstances ought to be reworked in the face of the radical challenge from the Muslim faith. In any case, the two messages, Qur'ān and gospel, seem quite irreconcilable on such essential points as the Trinity and the incarnation.

Here we come to the basic question: Can we speak of revelation after the New Testament? Would such an admission not be a requestioning of the fulness—some would say the absolute character—of God's revelation in Jesus Christ? How could we attribute to God texts that are so obviously "profane" and human, and consider them as expressions of God's Word? Especially, if God has spoken to us in God's Son Jesus Christ, can God yet speak in a manner so different, so incompatible with the gospel, so often contradictory to it? Can God revise divine judgments? Or must we find in the Qur'ān a different . . . and complementary Word, "another approach to the living God," to the mystery of God? But how can we set such a Word in the light of the gospel?

It is to these typical questions, and many others, that we would try to respond. But we must first of all examine the sources of our faith, the scripture and the tradition of the church (that of the fathers, the magisterium, and the theologians), in order to know whether and in what measure these sources of our faith may be favorable to the hypothetical recognition of an expression of revelation other than that of the Bible.

We Study the Bible

With a variety of literary genres and an editorial history of several centuries, the Old Testament is the written record of the witness of a people whose varied ethnic origin and political emergence remain unknown. This collection traces the development, sometimes at cross-purposes, of a stubborn attempt to recognize a God, named Yahweh, as its God and its only lord. In the same period as the theory and practice of empire were being developed in Mesopotamia, this "Israel" was subdued, exiled, and confronted by the theologies of a universalist tendency; Yahweh assumed the cosmic functions of a unique ruler of humankind (Genesis: the creation story). Theologies and perceptions of the world thus attest comprehensively to a faith in God the wise creator who is savior and liberator because of being the victorious master of chaos and every enemy, the supreme interpreter of the order of creation (and thus of every natural, political, and social order), absolutely free to call a people into existence and obedience in order to testify among the living that "God is God" and accessible to human acquaintance. The prophetic succession that runs the length of the Old Testament in the service of this call is kept in perpetual tension by the resistance of individuals and institutions. We can see today how the Deuteronomist theology of the "covenant" is only a specific instance of Israelite expressions of this difficult history: it cannot serve as a hermeneutic criterion for the entire Old Testament, even if it has an important editorial significance — its authors are among the first editor-censors to be aware of the corpus that the scribes and priests will revise during the exile and after the return — and even if its coherence is pleasing to the Western reader.

The closing centuries of the political history of the Judean kingdom threatened by the Greco-Roman empire and culture, would lead the Jews to read their scripture in the almost exclusive perspective of an affirmation of their ethnic election and the permanence of the promises that alone supported their hope of remaining as a people in Palestine. Even as the unified Mediterranean culture was expanding, however, certain groups came to recognize that wisdom (always revealed) was given "to all peoples in all times" (Ecclus. 24:6, 8). Besides, protests were raised against the prevailing ethnocentrism (Ruth, Jonah).

The Jesus of the Gospels claims in full the legacy of the grace of knowing God that the Israelites shared in the law and the prophets. Sent by the Father, he as a true son follows the paternal order in a perfect communion of will, thus fulfilling all the promises made to his people, which was called to turn the land with which it had been entrusted into one belonging to the poor, and to transform the law that had been revealed to it into a law to liberate persons from false powers and allow them a full measure of justice. John the Baptist, forerunner of the gospel, has already announced the radical abrogation of every privilege attached to racial or religious heritage, at the time of God's judgment. The gospel message itself is, as such, an invitation to the eschatological banquet, which no longer concerns only the prodigal children welcomed into the heart of the father, who is occasionally named as Abraham (Luke 16:19–31). Scenes like the ones that show the faith of the centurion who is without any doubt a Roman (Matt.

8:5–13 and parallels) or the allegiance of a "heretic" heathen like the Samaritan (Luke 10:29–37), mark out the narrative trail along which the gospel proclamation is traced, having taken the form of a variegated biography or an interpretation of the life and work of Jesus.

The Book of Acts and the older corpus of Pauline epistles bear witness to this radical breach in the wall of the fortress raised by the dominant Jewish reading around the texts of the Old Testament as a record of the promises inherent in the God of Israel. Because the Book of Acts is also a narrative, it offers a special illustration of this crisis, which gave birth to the polyethnic church charged with a message of reconciliation for all the known world of the time, notably to those who worship (as at Athens) an unknown God. Paul says this very concisely: "God was in Christ reconciling the world to Godself, no longer holding people's misdeeds against them, and God has entrusted us with the message of reconciliation" (2 Cor. 5:19).

What Christian Tradition Tells Us

AN OPENNESS TO OTHER REVELATIONS?

The New Testament and, following it, the fathers of the church (1st-7th centuries) were generally quite severe toward non-Christian ("pagan") religions. One must believe in Christ in order to be saved; "Nobody will enter the Kingdom of God unless they receive the name of the Son of God" (the pastor of Hermas, 2nd century, among many others) even though the (too) famous formula of St. Cyprian (3rd century) was originally aimed only at schismatics who knowingly broke with the structures of the church: "Outside the church there is no salvation."

However, many echoed the line taken by St. Paul on the possibility of knowing God through ways other than biblical revelation. These authors included within such knowledge a familiarity with the harmony of the world (M. Felix, 2nd century) and the self-awareness of humankind (Tertullian, 3rd century).

But "the delay of the incarnation" confronted the fathers with the question of the fate of humanity before the coming of Christ. The general reply was that "Christianity is as old as humanity." For the "inspired ones" of all times had already announced the Christ. They cited the sibyls, the "revelations" of Hermes Trismegistos, and especially the great philosophers of antiquity: Plato, Pythagoras, Aristotle, who were the first masters of truth for many of the fathers. Two authors have been particularly linked with this topic. St. Justin (2nd century), by playing on the meaning of *logos* (reason, and the Word of God), saw "fragments of seminal logos" in the arguments of the philosophers. St. Clement of Alexandria (2nd-3rd century) went the furthest. For him, philosophy was a "third testament" parallel to the Old Testament and not without links to it; philosophy, like the Old Testament, prepares the way for the New. It is a "propaedeutic" for faith in Jesus Christ, and "revelation extends beyond Judaism and Christianity."

St. Irenaeus of Lyons (late 2nd century) echoes St. Justin: his grandiose vision of the education of the human adult by divine pedagogy starts with an initial stage, represented by Adam, which involves obedience to natural law. But in the fourth century St. Augustine, who had on occasion been open to pre-Christian religions, would harden his stance after his struggle against Pelagianism, which extolled the role of human effort in the quest for truth and salvation. His pessimistic view of the *massa damnata* (the accursed mass of heathens) would cast a long shadow over the Christian tradition of the West.

From the Middle Ages to the middle of the twentieth century, theology was strongly influenced by St. Augustine, focusing on the problem of faith and grace in a particularly individual perspective. In the case of non-Christians, the problem was put in terms of the "unbelievers of good faith" symbolized by the "child raised in the forest." Since salvific faith must be "supernatural," it must respond to a revelation. It was generally supposed that God would send this "unbeliever" an angel or a missionary, or that they would benefit from a private revelation. But some writers took up the tradition regarding revelation accorded to the ancient philosophers Hermes Trismegistos and the sibyls (Abelard and others); St. Thomas Aquinas thought that certain great heathen minds had been aware of the truth and that all persons receive or refuse God's salvation according to their moral choices. Tostado, Bishop of Avila in the fifteenth century, acknowledged that pagans also had their prophets.

During the Renaissance, humanists like Erasmus (16th century) believed that Socrates, Plato, and even Cicero had been inspired by God. The Protestant reformers were divided between an openness to the humanist current (Zwingli, Bullinger) and their strong attachment to the Augustinian tradition (Luther). Calvin distinguished between a universal grace accorded by God to all persons and a special grace given only to the elect, those who believe in Jesus Christ; only the latter confers salvation.

Minority trends (mystics like Schwenckfeld, rationalists, or liberals like the Socinians and the Collegiants in Holland) wanted to follow the argument advanced by Nicholas of Cusa in his *De Pace Fidei* or Spinoza in his *Politico-Theological Treatise,* and gather all the religions around a common denominator. But the wave of Jansenism, even though it was condemned, was to stiffen theology in a manner that restricted the possibilities of salvation for Christians and a fortiori for non-Christians. However, the Jesuit De Ripalda (17th century) recognized a "broad faith" (*fides late dicta*) based on the simple witness of creation, and Jesuit missionaries in China tried vainly to win recognition for the teachings of Confucius.

With the Enlightenment (18th century), reaction against exclusivist teaching regarding faith and salvation evolved into a rational deism, open to anyone. This school of thought was mostly the work of a large group of Protestant thinkers and theologians (from John Locke to Leibnitz, Herder, and Schleiermacher), including some members of such movements for spiritual revival as the Quakers and the Moravian Brethren.

In the nineteenth century, fashion swung to the tradition and the survival among the heathen of traces of the primordial revelation to Adam (P. W. Schmidt). Félicité de Lamennais recognized that the heathens had their prophets. Up until the Second World War, there was little change. The unbelievers in good faith were attached to the soul of the church, but not its body. They were seen as minors in terms of moral or theological reasoning (Billot), and theologians revived the old theories about implicit faith, baptism of desire, the choice of the first free act, and the like. Distinctions were made among non-Christian religions between "building blocks" and "stumbling blocks." But, in the best of cases, they are only "crumbs that fall from the table."

During this time, Protestantism, like Roman Catholicism, sent missionaries to the four corners of the globe in the conviction that missionary work would prepare the world for the glorious return of Jesus Christ and his ultimate victory over the powers of unbelief and superstition. Protestant thinkers were sure of the superiority of the Christian religion over all others, even when they recognized their validity (A. Sabatier, E. Troeltsch, N. Söderblom).

This rapid historical survey allows us to measure the tensions that existed among persons who were certainly well-intentioned. Most of them, however, remained shut into their own system, in terms of both civilization and faith, in a world closed on itself (western Europe), which thought of moving out only to "discover" (an inappropriate and purely relative term) "new" worlds, in order to bring them the lights of reason and faith. This was a genuine, deep faith—this dispatch in mission involved an unlimited commitment which could lead to uprooting and even martyrdom—but a faith that considered itself to be absolute, unique, and exclusive. The fact that Roman Catholic theologians had to refer to "limbo," whither they consigned the "unbeliever in good faith," shows how embarrassed they were when confronted with what seemed to be the unfairness of birth (and of the call to baptism, the key to open the gates of salvation) in stark contradiction with the very notion of a just and good God who is love.

It was only after the Second World War and the collapse of Western colonialism that Christianity turned toward a genuinely positive appreciation of non-Christian religions and the need for friendly dialogue with them; from the first decade of the century, nevertheless, the work and action of Roman Catholics like Louis Massignon, Asin Palacios, and Monchanin, and Protestants like Maurice Leenhardt, Jean Faure, and Paul Tillich, and many others had revealed to Christians the values of the other religions.

The current of theology on non-Christian religions was really launched after the Second World War by Karl Rahner, R. Panikkar, G. Thils, P. Tillich, W. C. Smith, and J. Hick. As early as 1959, Rahner recognized the "legitimacy" of these religions as "positively desired by God" in the "general history of salvation" and "general revelation," which is to be distinguished from the "particular" or "special" revelation or history represented by Israel and Christianity. Its sign is the Noahic alliance (Gen. 9). These religions are the "ordinary" way of salvation for the vast majority of humanity and the charisma of their founders is a genuine revelatory prophecy, although "incomplete" (Cornélis), or "particular supernatural revelations" (J. P. Jossua).

The Second Vatican Council (1962–65) did not take a stand on the problem, but in its major texts and the *Declaration on the Relations of the Church to Non-Christian Religions (Nostra Aetate)* it indicated a positive openness to their values of faith and life. The many statements of the popes, especially Paul VI and John Paul II, and of the episcopates in the Third World have enlarged this opening, and the International Theological Conference at Nagpur, India (1971), affirmed that "the sacred scriptures and the religious rites and traditions on a world scale can, in varying degree, be expressions of a divine manifestation and lead to salvation."

The World Council of Churches is especially sensitive to the idea of a theology of dialogue and a community of communities based on the dialogue that God began in the earliest times with all humanity and on God's wish ultimately to gather all peoples into a single new humanity.

In 1961, at the New Delhi Assembly, the Indian theologian Paul Devanandan declared that the churches must recognize in the renaissance of non-Christian religions a creative act of the Holy Spirit in our history. The American theologian Joseph Sittler observed that the light of Christ could not be affirmed *against* any other lights.

In January 1971, Mgr. Georges Khodr vigorously addressed the WCC Central Committee and offered the contribution of the oriental churches. If Jesus Christ exercises his sovereignty directly over the church, he declared, there exists at the same time a mysterious and discrete economy of the Holy Spirit, which works within non-Christian religions and cultures, turning them in an appropriate manner toward the kingdom of God. The churches are called today to recognize this action of the Holy Spirit in the non-Christian religions and cultures, and allow themselves to be challenged by them.[2]

CHRISTIAN ATTITUDES TO THE QUR'ĀN

From its first appearance, Islam encountered Eastern Christianity, of which there are traces even in the text of the Qur'ān itself, but it was not until the middle of the eighth century that the Latin West began to take an interest in Islam.

The socio-political context is as important as doctrine in determining the Christian understanding of Islam and the Qur'ān. In this respect, the situation of the Eastern Christians—and, to a much lesser degree, those from the West—living inside the Islamic empire was radically different from that of the Christians who lived outside this empire. The former mixed, to a certain extent, with Muslims in their everyday life and they very soon spoke the same language, Arabic. Some of them held relatively important positions within administration: physicians (including the caliph's personal physician), philosophers, tax collectors, and financial administrators (Copts in Egypt), and even vizir to the caliph (Fatimid Egypt, 10th century). They enjoyed the status of "protégés" (*dhimmis*) but they were obviously regarded with a certain reserve. Their works are not lacking in justifications for Christian doctrines and practices, or even arguments for the superiority of Christianity over Islam, especially the excellence of Christian "law" (ethics) compared to Islamic law, and refutations of Muslim claims. But they carefully avoided anything that could seem blasphemous to the ears of their masters. They were more apologetic than polemic.

The cultural contribution of these Arab Christians of the Middle Ages was quite considerable and is too little known today, whether we refer to translations from the Greek tradition into Arabic, directly from Greek or through Syriac, of philosophy, medicine, or even Christian theology—for example, Yahya b. Adi's explanation of the Trinity (10th century). Works on the confrontation between Islam and Christianity, the Qur'ān and the gospel, were relatively abundant and many of them are still of relevance today.[3] They tried to explain Christian dogmas: Trinity, incarnation, redemption . . . in order to answer the objections of Muslims, with a remarkable effort at adaptation to the interlocutors, using their categories (e.g., the divine names and attributes) and willingly quoting from the Qur'ān. None went so far as recognizing the legitimacy of Islam after the advent of Christianity, of Muhammad after Jesus, or of the Qur'ān after the Gospels. But many recognized certain essential Islamic values: the oneness and transcendence of God, obedience to God's law, recognition of earlier prophets (even interpreting the title "word from God," which the Qur'ān attributes to Jesus, as an implicit recognition of his divinity), moral values, and so forth.

As examples of this openness, we note two particular writers. Timothy I, who was the Nestorian patriarch (Catholicos) of Baghdad in the early eighth century, had a "dialogue" with the Abbasi caliph al-Mahdi (late 781/ early 782).[4] The caliph asked him, "What then do you say about Muhammad?" Timothy replied. "He followed the way of the prophets." He then explained that by preaching the oneness of God, condemning idol-worship, fighting against polytheists (even the Byzantine Christians who were the Nestorians' hereditary enemies!), prescribing good and virtue and condemning evil and vice, Muhammad had acted like all the prophets. "So you believe in the prophet Muhammad!" declared the caliph. "I believe in one God, as the Torah, the Prophets, and the Gospel have taught me. But I believe that this God, one in divinity, is in three Persons," the patriarch concluded.

The other author is a Melkite bishop of the twelfth century, Paul of Antioch, who was probably bishop of Saida (Sidon). In his "Letter to a Muslim friend," he took great pains to show that the Qur'ān taught the same doctrine as Christianity, including the Trinity, for example in the formulation, "In the name of God, merciful, and compassionate," and that Christianity was genuinely monotheistic. He cited many qur'anic verses, although at times he took them out of context and twisted their meaning. The general tone of the letter is nevertheless irenic.[5]

Outside the Islamic empire, Christian countries were in almost continuous war with Islamic countries. The general attitude toward Islam and the Qur'ān was unavoidably conditioned by this situation. Very often, theological disquisitions sought to convince Christians of the doctrinal and moral perversions of the "infidels," to justify the defensive and offensive wars waged against them, and to kindle the courage of Christian soldiers.

We can distinguish two major groups of Christians confronted by Islam: the Byzantine world and the Latin West. Byzantine polemics were particularly negative, violent, and insulting.[6] From the time of St. John of Damascus (early 8th century), Muslims were called Ishmaelites or Hagarenes, with the object of excluding them from the covenant and legacy of Abraham by attaching them to the son of the bondwoman Hagar, and also Saracens ("expelled by Sarah"). They were infidels and idolaters: they worshiped in particular the black stone embedded in one corner of the Kaaba, the temple at Mecca; this stone was said to be the head of the goddess Aphrodite. The Qur'ān, used in apologetics to show the double nature of Christ, eternal divine Word and human speech, was nothing more than an incoherent jumble composed by Uthman, the third caliph. The few praiseworthy truths it contained were due to the monk Bahira, who was a Nestorian or an Arian. Finally, the Qur'ān and everything about Islam were the work of Satan and Muhammad was the Antichrist of the Apocalypse.

Until the Renaissance, the Latin West generally shared this negative viewpoint.[7] We can distinguish three major currents, which followed each other or even coexisted:

The first current is made up of legends from the Song of Roland to the Golden Legend of Jacques de Voragine and its *Roman de Mahon* (Muhammad). Mahon was the idol that Muslims worshiped along with Jupiter, Apollo, and Tervagant (the devil). At the beginning of the twelfth century, the Latin translation of the Qur'ān prepared under the auspices of Peter the Venerable, abbot of Cluny, introduced Westerners to a more exact understanding of the Qur'ān and Islam. But it also launched a series of apologetic and polemic "refutations," which would be developed from one generation to the next, sparing no affirmation of the Qur'ān in doctrinal or practical terms. As for Muhammad, he was only a false prophet (*pseudopropheta*) and an impostor; often he was portrayed as the Antichrist, the beast of the Apocalypse, or the devil incarnate.

We should, however, note some exceptions to this general indictment, in the works of several great minds like St. Thomas Aquinas, Raymond Lull, and especially Christians who had lived among Muslims and learned Arabic. Thus, in the thirteenth century William of Tripoli (modern Lebanon) put into relief the points common to Christianity and Islam, and concluded that Muslims were not far from the Christian faith. Ricoldo de Montecroce (14th century; a Dominican like William of Tripoli) was much more negative than William regarding the faith of Muslims. But he admired their piety, their faithfulness in prayer, and their hospitality, and he thought that Western Christians would do well to imitate them. His counsels of respect and humility for Christians who wanted to meet Muslims and his warning against controversy followed in a direct line from the "rules for brothers who are sent to Muslims" of St. Francis of Assisi (13th century). These are still utterly valid today. We should also mention the eleventh-century diplomatic letter of Pope Gregory VII to al-Nasir, the amir of Setif (in what is now modern Algeria), whom he called his "brother in Abraham," believer in the one God, creator of heaven and earth.[8] In the fourteenth century, John Wycliff, an Oxford theologian, compared the spirit of the gospel to the spirit of the Qur'ān and acknowledged that Muslims could be saved.

The third current was that of cultural exchanges. Occurring mostly during the relatively peaceful periods of coexistence, notably in Spain and Sicily (kingdom of Naples), this current opened to the West an awareness of the Greek scientific and philosophic heritage as it was articulated and enriched by Arab-Muslim science; this new awareness nurtured the intellectual awakening of medieval Europe from the twelfth to the fourteenth century. It is not without reason that people match the beginning of modern times with the arrival in the Latin world of Averroism and its autonomy of reason (the two ways to truth).

At the close of the Middle Ages, with the coming of Renaissance humanism (15th-16th centuries) and its climate of concordism between Plato and Aristotle), there was a wave of essays of "concord" between religions, like *De Pace Fidei* by Cardinal Nicholas of Cusa (1401–1464). At the same time, the line of refutations of the Qur'ān was continued by the same Nicholas of Cusa (*Cribatio Alchorani*, 1461), John of Segovia, Denis the Carthusian (*Contra perfidiam Machumeti*, 1460), and others. But knowledge of the Qur'ān improved and reached a sort of culmination with the monumental work of Ludovico Marracci whose very faithful Latin translation of the Qur'ān, accompanied by the commentary of Baydawi and a long prologue refuting the errors of the Qur'ān (Padua, 1698) would long remain the principal authority. At this time, too, appeared the first translations of the Qur'ān into European vernaculars, notably French (Du Ryer, 1647), English (A. Ross, 1648; G. Sale, 1734), Italian (A. Arrivabene, 1543), German (S. Schweigger, 1616), and Dutch (Glazemaker, 1658).

The openness of Renaissance humanism was succeeded by that of the Enlightenment (18th century). The vague, rationalizing deism of this era claimed to find its model in the Qur'ān and Islam; but we must not forget that this esteem for Islam was also part of the struggle to "crush infamy" on the part of the French (Catholic) philosophers of the time, especially Voltaire. In his biography of Muhammad (1730) the count of Boulainvilliers saw the Prophet as a prototype of the free thinker, preaching a natural and reasonable religion. Setting aside diplomatic motives, we know the profound thought and attitudes of Bonaparte in Egypt (1798). This positive yet ulterior interest was extended by the romantic exoticism of the nineteenth century and Thomas Carlyle, a specialist on hero worship and the role of heroes in history (1841), found Muhammad to be an illustration of the heroism under study.

But for three centuries these open attitudes revealed more about Western ideas and literature than specifically Christian thinking. Whether Catholic, Protestant, or Orthodox, this has remained obstinately shut against any values articulated by the Qur'ān. We could even say that the depreciation of Islam reached its peak in the nineteenth century, through a change in form. In the eyes of the moralizing religion of this period, Islam appeared as absolute immorality, with polygamy, repudiation of one's wife at will, the sensuous joys of paradise, and a thousand other turpitudes, many of them invented. The few values that could be discerned (notably monotheism) had been borrowed or "stolen" from biblical tradition. Finally, Islam was a "trick of Satan" clothed in a semblance of truth, the better to seduce believers and fling them into error.

We would have to wait until the second half of the twentieth century to see this current reversed: only then did the work of a few pioneers from the beginning of the century find a virtually universal resonance, principally in the position on Islam adopted by the Second Vatican Council (1962–65).

We can reasonably be astonished at such a long and insistent hardness of heart within most Christian thinking about Islam. But we must remember that religious ideas are molded by historical circumstances and often by strategic considerations as well. For ten centuries, the Muslim world was the only rival and often the enemy of the Christian world, even after the great discoveries. Should we be astonished, then, if its religion, Islam, appeared as *the* virtually unique non-Christian and even anti-Christian religion par excellence?

We have already mentioned the role of the pioneers at the beginning of the twentieth century in reversing the Christian attitude toward non-Christian religions in general. With reference to Islam, two names already noted are of special importance. The first is that of the Spanish priest and orientalist Miguel Asin Palacios (1871–1944). He never directly addressed the theological problem of the religious merit of Islam and the Qur'ān, but his copious writings imply a positive judgment, by the way he treats Islamic theology and mysticism as sources in relation to these same disciplines in Christianity, even though he occasionally somewhat "christianizes" Muslim authors.[9]

But the decisive influence was that of Louis Massignon (1883–1962).

Brought back to the faith of his childhood during an ordeal near Baghdad in 1908 and "visited" by grace in the form of a Muslim friend, he dedicated his whole life to telling the Christian world about the greatness of Islam, principally seen through Islamic mysticism. His scientific writings on sufism, beginning with his magisterial thesis *La passion de Hallaj, martyre mystique de l'Islam* (Paris, 1922, 2 vols.; 2nd ed., 1975, 4 vols.), are still authoritative today. They revealed to Christian theologians mystical experiences of such intensity that they inevitably posed the problem of their inspiration: the Qur'ān. Massignon refused to call himself a theologian, but he expressed himself several times on this point. For him, Islam was the "providential" resurgence of the line of Abraham through his own son Ishmael, the excluded one. Muhammad was a "negative prophet" in the sense, it would seem, that he denied what God was not. To train Christians in their spiritual approach to Islam, Massignon founded (1934) at Damietta a "league" of prayers, the *Badalīyah* (prayer of substitution), which would eventually reach into the highest levels of the Roman Church. We would have to include in Massignon's following virtually every Christian—or at least Roman Catholic—student of Islam of the past fifty years: J. M. Abdeljalil (1904–1979), Louis Gardet (1904–1986), G. C. Anawati, et al.

The texts from Vatican II that consider Islam are unquestionably the fruit of this new tendency. One could quote here the opening words of the major text of the *Declaration on the Relationship of the Church to Non-Christian Religions* (*Nostra Aetate*), paragraph 3: "The church looks with favor on the Muslims." Banal as they may seem, these words give expression to this radical change of attitude. The council adopted no theological position on Islam—such was not its goal—but it mentioned in a positive way the essential Islamic dogmas and rites, in order to invite Christians and Muslims to a fraternal dialogue and a common commitment to the service of humankind.

Since Vatican II, this tendency has continued to develop, in spite of the hesitations and anxieties in certain quarters. Numerous statements by recent popes, notably Paul VI and John Paul II, indicate a certain progress in this direction,[10] with what one could consider to be an apex: John Paul II's speech to the Christians of Ankara (November 1979), in which he called them to a genuine "spiritual brotherhood" with Muslims.[11] The same can be said of comments by members of the Roman Catholic hierarchy, such as the inaugural lecture of Cardinal Tarancon, archbishop of Madrid and then president of the Spanish Catholic Bishops' Conference, to the Second Christian-Muslim Conference of Córdoba (March 1977); on this occasion he called on Christians to recognize Muhammad's prophetic tone, especially his faith in one God and his thirst for justice.[12]

On the Protestant side, we can trace the same evolution. There are many authors: W. Cantwell Smith, W. Montgomery Watt, and especially the Anglican bishop Kenneth Cragg, whose most recent work, *Muhammad and the Christian: A Question of Response* (London and Maryknoll, N.Y., 1984) calls on Christians to recognize without quibbling that Muhammad was really a prophet while still insisting that Jesus was "more than a prophet." Among the Orthodox there are fewer writers, but Mgr. Khodr (already noted) and Olivier Clément, who attributes an eschatological role to Islam, are moving in the same direction.[13]

Our suggestions would extend this general movement, although they represent, in our view, a new step forward.

Our Suggestions

We shall begin by trying to find *criteria* that would enable Christian faith to recognize the Word of God in scripture other than the Bible. Then we shall examine *the case of the Qur'ān*. There are a number of *Christian attitudes* that could be adopted, some of which are more or less widely held, concerning the Qur'ān. As we proceed, we shall likely provoke a number of spontaneous objections in the minds of our Christian readers, and we shall try to answer these.

IN SEARCH OF CRITERIA OF AUTHENTICITY FOR NON-CHRISTIAN REVELATION

It is a delicate task to establish Christian criteria for discerning whether something that presents itself as a revelation of the Word of God outside the biblical context is really what it claims to be. Some say it is impossible. It is true that there is a constant risk of absolutizing what is only secondary or instrumental in Christian faith; for example, the Greek categories by which the Christian faith has historically been defined. This has often been done. Nevertheless, if we believe that our faith is a light from the grace of God, and the most intense light possible, it should at least try to account for the realities of our world, and especially to make sense of that great religious movement that is Islam. Bearing this case in mind, along with those of other non-Christian religions, we can prepare certain criteria.

We have not retained an early criterion, which would have considered the authenticity of the experience of God related by persons who present themselves as transmitters of a revelation in the name of God; for example, the experience of God cited by Muhammad. On the one hand, the circumstances of his personal and religious life come to us mainly via the *hadiths*. Now the critics of *hadith*, whether Muslims or Orientalists, know how difficult it is to sift the authentic from the apocryphal in this immense literature. The only really sure data are those mentioned in *the text* of the Qur'ān, and these are very few. On the other hand, good Christian theology of prophethood reminds us that it is not the personal holiness of prophets that determines the truth of their message, but the content of the message itself.[14] We thus arrive at the modern approach to semantics: everything derives from the text. This in no way questions the historicity of the Prophet, the importance of his role, the impact of his cultural milieu, or the quality of his religious experience. Simply stated, we learn about him through the text of the Qur'ān.

It is therefore the *content of the message* — about God, humanity, the relationship between God and human persons and the relations between persons — that will be our *first criterion*. But every criterion presupposes a frame of reference. What should ours be? That is the crucial problem.

The usual response is the following: the criterion of conformity or congruence — and not just noncontradiction — with the Christian message. We can readily understand the reasons behind such a criterion, which essentially concerns the coherence of the Christian faith with itself. If we believe that God spoke to us in Jesus Christ, how could we recognize another word about God that did not conform to the Word that is the basis of our faith, which would be different, even contradictory, or in any case irreconcilable with it? "God cannot contradict God."

This idea of revelation has given rise to an abundant literature on the "Christian values of non-Christian religions." It amounts to choosing from within the other religions whatever appears to conform to Christian doctrines and practices, and to seeing in these the "building blocks" (which we have already mentioned) for a full approach to faith in Jesus Christ.

We do not deny the legitimacy of this approach in the mind of many Christians. But for our part we have no intention of shutting ourselves within it. In the first place, our experience has shown us how offensive this view is to our Muslim friends. This "recovery" of the values of their religion on the basis of our categories, this cleavage that we put between what is "valid" and what is not, seems to them to insult their faith and their religious life. But that would not be an adequate reason for ignoring this idea if it was the only option for Christian faith and bound in essence to that faith.

What is essential to Christian faith is to believe that the risen Christ, "received into the glory of the Father," is mysteriously present at the core of world history and the history of every person. But for all that, we would not make of every sincere believer an "anonymous Christian" (a very questionable term invented by Karl Rahner). The current orientation of the theology of non-Christian religions, which owes much to Rahner himself, allows us (we believe) to broach the problem in a different way, which is also based on scripture, as we have shown.

In the context of "general revelation," God has not ceased to manifest Godself to humans since the beginning of humanity. Nor will God cease to do so until the end of the human race. Even in the context of "special revelation," God has chosen to make God's Word move slowly among humans. At first (some millennia after the appearance of humans on earth) the Word moved with a small nation, Israel, crushed between empires. Then it moved with a man, Jesus, who never left Palestine and who died three years (at the most) after he had begun to proclaim his gospel. Although the gospel of the risen one has been proclaimed for twenty centuries through the known world, more than four-fifths of humanity is still unaware of it. Can we think that God has left the vast majority of humans, in time and space, without communicating with them in any way?

Besides, as we have said, every "Word of God"—an unavoidably anthropomorphic expression to designate the "self-communication" of God to humanity—passes through human expression. No human expression of the Word of God, even in the special form that Christians recognize in Jesus Christ and Muslims in the Qur'ān, can claim, by definition, to exhaust the mystery of God or represent the entirety of God's Word.

It is this limitation of every human expression of the Word of God, to say nothing of human sin, that can, we believe, explain the divergences between revelations. It is not God who is self-contradictory, but those who speak in God's name. A comparison of several passages from the Old and New Testaments will suffice to illustrate this phenomenon. That is why we feel no need to retain the criterion of measuring every revelation in terms of the revelation in Jesus Christ as it has been transmitted by the Apostles and the church.

But, many Christians will say, has God not said everything to us in Jesus Christ, the very Word of God made human? Indeed, many expressions of the New Testament and church tradition have such a resonance: "In Christ you have all enrichment, both in knowledge and expression. . . . There is no gift which you lack" (1 Cor. 1:5–7); "In him, you have been brought to completion" (Col. 2:10); "We have all received of his fulness" (John 1:16). The faith of the apostolic tradition to which the New Testament bears witness is surely that it is the very Word of God, incarnate in Jesus Christ, who has spoken to us (John 1:1–14).

All this is incontestably essential to Christian faith. But we can understand these New Testament texts as affirming that faith in Christ brings fulness of life, without necessarily going so far as to insist that revelation in Jesus Christ is the *absolute* (Hegel's word) revelation and even exclusive of any other. Some remarks are in order:

1. In the strictest of terms, only God is absolute.

2. In Jesus Christ, God made man according to Christian faith, the relationship between God and humanity by "hypostatic" union has reached its apogee. The Jesus Christ event cannot be surpassed.

3. *What is said to us* about God and this Jesus Christ event is said to us *in human language*. The words of Jesus, even those uttered by his person who is the Word of God—and thus endowed with a uniquely "theandric" character—are human words, situated in time and place, and by definition inadequate to express the totality of the eternal Word of God and the singular mystery of his person as incarnate Word.

4. Finally, the Gospels and other New Testament writings have only transmitted to us a portion of these words and signs of Jesus, as St. John himself has said (John 20:30; 21:31). What has been said is enough for us

to "believe that Jesus is the Christ, the Son of God, and ... believing we may have life in his name" (John 20:31).

We could add two other degrees of relativity (which is always to be distinguished from relativism). For one, if scripture is closed for Christians, its *meaning* is not totally unveiled. It will be so only at the end of time (the Parousia) and the church is continuously discovering it. Also, the communication of the Word of God by Christian scripture is burdened with relativizing elements, which pertain to all communication in human speech: the witness of the life of Christ or the inspired prophet (writer-articulator-narrator) has transmitted the message in the structures of thought and expression appropriate to a particular context of time and place, which are no longer those of readers through the ages; these are different from the original auditors, contemporaries of the scripture. The later readers must bear all the components of every act of reading. Reading itself is affected by modes of speech and action in its own context, and also by the weight of earlier readings that tradition has passed on. Thus a divergence develops between what is said and what is perceived, and this conditions the received meanings of the message.

This does not at all lead to relativism, agnosticism, or indifference. Across these human expressions of the mysteries of God and Christ, the faith of the believer truly reaches the person of Christ and, through him, God in the fulness of divinity. This must be true of any authentic faith, according to the fine formula of St. Thomas Aquinas; *actus credentis non terminatus ad enuntiabile sed ad rem* (the act of faith does not end with the formula—of Jesus, scripture, church, or our personal ideas—but at the very reality of God).[15] We should even say that the quality of a faith is not measured by the exactness of its formulation; God knows how poor our faith would be in such a situation! How rich, too, can be the faith of simple persons who reach the mystery without passing through intelligence and formulation!

Moreover, for the Christian, the revelation of God in Jesus Christ is the deepest expression possible of divine mystery and human destiny, "God's last word about any religious quest," as certain contemporary theologians would say. This is so not only in a subjective sense for the Christian, but objectively for every person. But this revelation is neither absolute nor exclusive.

What remains, then, of the criterion of the content of the message? The answer, we believe, lies in the quality of the message about God and humanity, inevitably perceived through the eye of Christian experience (otherwise, we should renounce all sense of vision in faith). But we must not demand another expression of "revelation" to be "purer" than the Bible; nor may we judge everything according to the standard of Christian doctrine.

The other criterion that seemed essential to us relates to the *fruitfulness of the message among humans.* "We judge the tree by its fruit." It should therefore be possible to recognize, in the individual and collective life of persons of today and yesterday, the influence of the message; what we could call the fruits of holiness. But we cannot require more of a non-Christian message than we ask of the gospel. However pure it may be, fruitfulness is filtered through thick layers of shadows, of obstacles all too human, in Christianity as elsewhere. The church is composed of sinners, who sometimes become saints, and who at least must always strive to become so. The essential seems to be to rediscover in every authentic religious message a permanent urging to holiness, and some attainments to this holiness in varying degrees.

THE EXPERIENCE OF GOD AT THE ORIGIN OF THE QUR'ĀN

We begin by observing that reading the Qur'ān – if possible in its original language – reveals a deep experience of God to the Christian who approaches the task without prejudice. There are cries that do not deceive. Of course, such an experience, like any experience religious or not, escapes the bounds of definition, for the person concerned, for contemporaries, and even more for those at a distance. It reveals itself as it expresses itself, in a language often poetic or lyric. The Qur'ān bears such unmistakable hallmarks. We could add many other indices, like the refusal to "prove" anything, to reply to polytheists who want proofs or miracles, when it can only affirm and proclaim what it has "seen" (Qur'ān 53:1–18; 81:15–24, etc.)

We could surely find other explanations for this religious experience that we perceive through the text of the Qur'ān, for these have not been in short supply: explanations of a human, sociological, psychological, even pathological order. Much could be said of them, especially about the naivety of "scholars" who use only material that suits their case. What is at stake for us is the divine "government" of the world. We could not admit that an experience and a message of such quality and fruitfulness could be the result of an interplay of solely human factors, with God remaining passive and indifferent to the process.

The Content of the Message Delivered

The reflections of the Christians mentioned at the beginning of this chapter have already noted the principal religious, doctrinal, and ethical dimensions of the Qur'ān. Here we shall underline only the axial one, which informs all the others: the oneness of the transcendent God.

The oneness of God is not just the negation of a numerical plurality of gods. It is the affirmation that everything comes from God and returns to God, in this life and the beyond. Everything receives its existence and its life from the eternal God and everything exists in relation to God. God is the very source of all human life, religious and sometimes mystical as it may be.

This unique, transcendent God is radically different and apart from every creature, particularly humans. It is to be noted that transcendence in no way implies remoteness. The "distant God of Islam," an expression frequently used by Christians, is a contradiction in terms. God is "near" to humanity, as the Qur'ān insists, as it unceasingly calls humanity to draw near to God.

That is why the attitude appropriate to a person is first of all worship: recognition of God's universal lordship, respect for God's rights and the rights God has given to creatures, rejection of all idols ancient and modern, the doing of God's will in all fields of human activity, the need for continual conversion and turning to God.

Christians have learned to read all these attitudes into the person of Jesus of Nazareth, a true son of Israel (see Matt. 22:37–40). Without doubt, the unique relationship between Jesus and his Father would be, for the Christian faith, the revelation of the person of Jesus as the eternal Son of this Father and of the mystery of the one God in three persons. But despite a thousand difficulties, this radical monotheism and this transcendence of God are never brought into question, either in Jesus or in Christian tradition.

But those Christians who know the Qur'ān will immediately say, the Qur'ān does not stop at an affirmation of the oneness of God. It also denies "the God of Jesus Christ," reproaching Christians for saying "three" with reference to God (4:171, 5:73) and making Jesus (and his mother?) a divinity beyond the one God (4:71, 5:17, 116–17, etc.), to say nothing of the repudiation of the crucifixion (4:156). For a long time it has been noticed that the formulations of the dogmas so denied are not those of the orthodox faith and could not therefore diminish it. Some have even gone as far as to say that the negation of false formulations would implicitly confirm the true. Without falling into this latter excess, we could well retain the preceding comment. But to do so would be to forget the central message of the Qur'ān. Beyond the specific denials, more or less well formulated, it is this central message of the Qur'ān, the oneness of the transcendent God according to the qur'anic confession, that entails the denial of the incarnate God and the rejection of the triune God. We stand here in the presence of a common faith in a unique and transcendent God, but according to two diverse and irreconcilable conceptions of monotheism. We shall return to this problem later on.

Other objections, which were also raised by the Christians in our group, concern the evidence in the Qur'ān of very human problems felt to be incompatible with the Word of God. The answer to this point seems easy enough. First of all, Christians could here betray a strabismus, which afflicts others as well, by forgetting that they continuously draw nourishment from a scripture (the Old Testament) that is packed with very human passions, cries of war and vengeance, even in the most beautiful psalms. This hardly prevents us from proclaiming at the end of every reading, "the Word of the Lord"! Jesus himself, although without sin, knew human passion, tenderness, and violence. And the Apostles and early Christians were hardly angels.

More deeply we need only apply the principle whereon we have reached agreement: revelation is always indirect: the Word of God, which always passes through human beings, does not suppress, in those who transmit the revelation, the limitations or imperfections that are the lot of the human condition. *There is no Word of God or divine scripture in the pure state*, but there are expressions of the Word of God across modes of speech and action specifically human.

In the case of Christian revelation, Jesus Christ himself, eternal Word of God in his person according to the Christian faith, only expressed the mystery of God and his own mystery across specifically human modes of speech and action. A fortiori, the Christian scriptures, which transmit his message, are therefore not in themselves words of God in the pure state — that is, without human mediation.

In the case of the Qur'ān, we recognize an expression of the Word of God, but this does not mean that we adhere to the Muslim idea that the whole Qur'ān, to the minutest detail, was dictated verbatim by God to the Prophet, with or without the interposition of the angel Gabriel. But we also refuse to sift what may seem pure to us from the impure, what suits us from what we do not like. It is the entire Qur'ān that is marked by the Word of God, but within the limitations set by human mediation. Muslims have the task of distinguishing what is essential from what is not, and this has varied and will continue to vary according to the context and requirements of each era and even of each believer.

Our group reflected especially on the many qur'anic verses that deal with problems of a judicial or, more generally, temporal nature. We noticed that the Bible has just as many. Some of us thought that they were of no more interest to us than was Leviticus. Others, however, stressed the importance of this dimension, in both the Qur'ān and the Bible, for reminding every believer that faith imposes requirements and that it must be carried into all of life. The "unique commandment" of Jesus Christ, to love to the point of laying down one's life for one's friends, is not, or at least should not be, any less exigent.

One final objection was put forward: How could the Qur'ān be the Word of God if it brings nothing new (except deviations) to the Bible and even appears to some Christians as a "regression toward the Old Testament"?

We should first of all note that the Qur'ān does not present itself as a novelty (*bid'*, 46:9, referring to the Prophet), but as a repetition, a reminder (*dhikr*) of earlier revelations. As for reducing the Qur'ān to its sources, this is an operation that is as unsatisfying for the Qur'ān as for the Bible — not only the Old Testament, which draws heavily on earlier or contemporaneous religious traditions, but also the New Testament, as we now know better than before. Besides, no text can be explained by its sources, but only by the use it makes of them in its own perspective and idiom.

Finally, a revelation or a prophecy is not defined by its "novelty." The prophet, God's spokesperson, is one who arises in a given milieu in given circumstances, usually in a crisis, and who vividly reminds others of the will of God.

It is precisely in this "crisis," in the "subversive" nature of the message in relation to ossified traditions, that we can say that it has a prophetic character.

The Fruitfulness of the Message

This can be observed in three facets. First there is the passage of part of humankind from polytheism to monotheism, not only in seventh-century Arabia, but still today. Then there are the treasures of religion and spiritual life that can be at least partially perceived in more than thirteen centuries of Islamic literature. In general, we immediatly think of Islamic mysticism or sufism. This is true even though the term "sufism" covers a variety of phenomena from *hajj* to the religious orders, and even though the relationship between sufism and Islamic "orthodoxy" has not been simple (less simple indeed than is often supposed) but subject to important modifications. Still, it remains part of the heritage of Islam and, in several cases, what we know of it reveals the most exalted religious experience, born and nourished, by the grace of God, through the meditation of the Qur'ān. But we also refer to the "ordinary" religious life, which is fed by the beliefs and rituals of a most classic nature and which permeates the life of sincere Muslims, the "just qadis," leaders who care for the common good, citizens who risk their life to protest against the injustice of those in authority. This authentic permeation of the message in the life of today's Muslims — beyond doubt the most important of our "aspects" — can be discerned in a number of writings. It is especially evident to those who have formed friendships with certain Muslims and have been able to catch a glimpse of their deepest sentiments. Here, too, there is no question of defining or even describing, but simply of communicating this acute feeling, so often encountered, that this life and these profound attitudes, whether or not they derive directly from the Qur'ān, cannot be based on an illusion. That would be an insult to the life of believing Muslims, and even more so to divine providence. In brief, the Qur'ān has sustained, and continues to sustain today, an immense cry of faith in the one God, which has considerable weight in the contemporary world and which must find its place in every Christian reflection about the "divine plan for salvation" and especially about revelation.

But there are Christians who will find this fruitfulness of the Qur'ān very ambiguous, even if they do not consider the Qur'ān and Islam to be responsible for the past and present trials and misfortunes of Christendom. Some evoke the destruction of entire provinces of the Christian world in the early centuries of Islam, the declarations of "holy war," the current expansion of Islam in Africa south of the Sahara and even in the West, and all this shuts many hearts to any talk of a higher truth.

Let us remark that the same sort of talk is heard on the Muslim side, in an inverse perspective, of course, but with the same good reasons. Is it really necessary to step into this field mined with passion? Let us simply point the way to what should be a program of impartial study. To begin, we should twist the necks of a number of "myths" ("holy war," "believe or die"). Then, we should make a historical balance sheet that will show beyond question that the excesses have been at least evenly distributed, like the sins of believers. Finally, we should compare the "sources," especially the New Testament and the Qur'ān, to establish the "difference," particularly with reference to the use of violence.

But it is enough to recall something that nobody can doubt: the spiritual appeals, which are the essence of the Qur'ān, now as always. Neither of our religions is without dark patches. Only God can divide the light from the shadows.

All this leads Christians to a decision that does not clearly derive from logical argument, but is the fruit of a free exercise of faith. They can (we feel) legitimately recognize the Qur'ān as a scripture that expresses a Word of God, not only for the Muslim, but also for the Christian and every human being.

But the challenge that necessarily confronts a Christian, once that has been accepted, is to try to account for this phenomenon on the basis of one's own faith, of the specifically Christian vision of the divine "economy" or the divine plan for salvation. This can be done only through the integration of two basic truths: the original place of Christianity in this divine plan, which the fathers called the *novitas christiana* (Christian novelty); and what we have just said about the presence of a divine revelation in the phenomenon of the Qur'ān. Here indeed is what was expected of our group and our work. As we said at the outset, this is a very difficult question, which has as yet hardly been explored, but it cannot be avoided. We shall be led to ask more questions of the Christian faith than the clean, clear answers that we can offer.

In order to respect this margin of uncertainty, we shall here suggest several types of solutions, or rather several possible Christian approaches to this dilemma. Consciously or not, they derive from different theological or religious lineages.

SOME POSSIBLE APPROACHES

An Existential Approach

We referred to this in the common introduction to this third part. It consists of concretely experiencing the contradiction without being able for the moment to overcome it with a broader perspective. So for Christians it is a matter of fully living according to their own scripture, endlessly discovering its infinite richness, particularly in a familiarity and even a certain communion with the faith of others, and, at the same time, recognizing the validity and divine origin of the scriptures by which their Muslim friends live. This involves a renunciation, at least provisional, of any attempt to put these two visions of truth into a coherently packaged divine plan of the sort we have derived from our own scripture.

This approach is fairly common. It is often linked with an intense spiritual life and a genuine communion with the faith of others. It can also be found together with a radical mistrust of all "indiscreet" theology, or even all theology of any kind. But it is also encountered in the form of an attitude of waiting, which does not exclude—indeed even hopes for—a theological proposition that would at least offer an attempt at a synthesis.

This approach is eminently respectable, imbued with a profond respect for the mystery of God and God's Word, but it is not in itself very different from others which try to go further into theological reflection; it is to these that we must now turn.

A "Classical" Approach

This term is meant to indicate a Christian approach based on "classical" theology; some would call it "scholastic," but we intend no pejorative nuance in either case. We refer simply to the theology of St. Thomas Aquinas and his school, which is still very much alive.

This approach has its beginnings in one of several comments of St. Thomas on prophecy,[16] in which he distinguishes two types of revelation, corresponding to the two ends of prophecy: to make known the divine truth and to "direct human action." In 1956 Charles Ledit suggested[17] the application of this second type of prophecy and revelation to the case of the Qur'ān, which might have brought nothing that was not already known but sustained a powerful movement toward known truths.

One eminent Thomist went further: the late Cardinal Charles Journet, who had often considered the problem from different perspectives. He admitted in 1960 that Muhammad could have benefited from a partial prophetic light (*lumen propheticum*) that vividly illuminated the monotheism of the transcendent God without reaching other truths, which either remained in the shadows or were denied outright.[18]

One of our number had developed a similar vision, also in 1960. Building on the analysis of Yves Congar,[19] he accepted the Qur'ān as a revelation, but one that was not "contributory" to the revealed corpus (which had been closed at the death of the last Apostle), nor "officially explanatory" (which is the role of the magisterium), nor properly speaking "spiritually explanatory" (as is the case with the persons of great inspiration within the church), but in an "analogous" way, outside Christianity and "partial," because it contains part of the truth.[20]

There is no objection against these "classical" attitudes from the point of view of Roman Catholic orthodoxy. But one could wonder whether they account fully for the unity of the Qur'ān, or whether they do not chop it into pieces in order to make it fit the categories of classical theology. By analogy, if we applied these categories to the Old Testament, we could recognize as revealed only what conformed to the gospel and the teachings of the church. Not much would survive.

Some of us also warned against the harmful consequences that a "theology of exclusion" could have on certain minds and certain practical attitudes. In any case, there is no question here of condemning anyone, but we wish to note the progress in theological reflection that (we believe) enables us to situate the problem in a broader perspective.

A Broadening of Revelation as History and Meaning

As we have already noted, Christian theology of revelation before the mid-twentieth century had accepted, with few exceptions, as an expression of the Word of God only the Bible culminating in Jesus Christ, incarnate Word of God, whose gospel was transmitted by the writings of the New Testament, which were themselves interpreted by the church. In the Protestant tradition, the doctrine of Luther and Barth prevailed: outside faith in Jesus Christ, there is only impiety. The Roman Catholic tradition seemed to have stopped at the "close of revelation" at the death of the last Apostle[21] without considering the context, which shows clearly that what is closed is the corpus of the New Testament, which tells us of the Word of God in Jesus Christ.

One the one hand, we have seen that, from the very beginning of human life on earth, God has consistently "spoken," and continues to "speak," to humans in many ways. On the other hand, we reach the revelation in Jesus Christ only through the texts of the New Testament, which reveal *meaning* until the end of time. The church awaits this culmination, remaining attentive to the questions continually raised by the events of history, in which Christians necessarily participate. As it waits, the church rereads its own scripture, drawing new meanings from it, which enable it to answer the questions of our contemporaries. Among these events, an important place is taken by the birth, development, and continued presence of Islam.

It is certainly not our intention to adopt current fashions or to take the easy path by favoring Muslim-Christian dialogue at any price. On the contrary, we believe that our approach is faithful to the requirements of truth imposed by the data of history and our present age. It leads us on the one hand to consider the experiences of Christians who have had genuine relationships with Muslims, and so been led to look afresh at their scripture, their tradition, and the formulation of certain dogmas. On the other hand, we feel called to question a set of evidence that is of relative validity and seek the enduring essence under the accretions of history in order to translate it into an accessible idiom. In short, we would live more deeply in a faith that has been cleansed, renewed, and enriched by a different religious experience.

This Christian experience can be situated within the perspectives opened by the Christian theology of non-Christian religions, which we have already mentioned. This is characterized by two dimensions. First, there is a recognition of "general" revelation, by which God has communicated and continues to communicate with humanity, from the first appearance of human beings on earth until its end; the great religions are, in various forms, the setting for this manifestation. Also, and as a consequence, there is a new consideration of these religions as a whole, with their shadows and lights, regardless of the subjective intentions of individuals who can be saved by a personal grace expressed in terms of an upright conscience.

In our reflection on scripture, we therefore consider the Qur'ān (and Islam) as an entity, just as we consider any scripture, wherein each element (even those that appear secondary, too human, or even opposed to the Word of God in Jesus Christ) plays its inalienable role in a coherent totality. In the Qur'ān, everything is in fact oriented to the proclamation of the oneness of God: the vision of history, the perception of the world, the religious and temporal prescriptions both individual and social. These are all but refractions and inferences from this central message. It is therefore as a function of this principal axis that our Christian perspective is focused on the Qur'ān.

That being said, the broadening of revelation can take two forms: a reminder of our own revelation, and a recognition of another expression of the Word of God, with all that differentiates it from the Word of God in Jesus Christ.

An examination of our own revelation was clearly and publicly stated by one of our members during a meeting of Muslims and Christians:

When we affirm that Christians do not believe in the prophet Muhammad, it is important to understand the meaning of this statement. Without a doubt, as Christians, we cannot bring ourselves to see Muhammad as the end and seal of prophecy. Indeed for us revelation finds its culmination in the person of Jesus Christ. And Jesus is more than a prophet: as the Son of God, he is the unsurpassable event as God's presence among human beings.

But that does not stop us from giving the prophet Muhammad and the Qur'ān as a sacred book a privileged status in relation to the other revelations and religious traditions of humanity. Personally, as a Christian theologian but without wishing to commit my Christian brothers, I have no hesitation in saying that the revelation of which Muhammad is the messenger is *a* Word of God, which addresses me in my faith. I do not say that the Qur'ān is *the* Word of God, but I willingly say that the Qur'ān contains a confession of faith in God that concerns me as a Christian and calls me therefore to consider Muhammad as an authentic witness of the God in whom I believe. Within our three religious traditions we are all children of Abraham. That is why I feel I can say that Muhammad, the Qur'ān, and the religious history of Islam as a repository of treasures of prayer, love, and justice have a special place in the salvation history that began with Abraham and will finish at the end of the human race.

If I am now asked why as a Christian I take an interest in Islam, I happily reply that Islam is for me a prophetic reminder of Israel's original confession of faith: you shall worship one God. The qur'anic revelation calls me to reread the biblical revelation that finds its fulfilment in Jesus Christ, emphasizing the absolute nature of the one God and keeping myself from any sin of idolatry.[22]

This understanding of the Qur'ān as a receptacle of a Word of God that refers Christians (and Jews) to the Word they receive in their own scripture introduces an explicit relationship between the qur'anic revelation and the prophetic history that began with Abraham and developed in the three branches of monotheism: Jewish, Christian, and Muslim. We realize that each of these three religions defines its relationship to Abraham in a different way, believing itself to benefit from a privileged link with him and situating the other two accordingly. This is what sets the specificity of each of our religions and we intend to respect it.

Still, despite their differences, the three monotheisms share a faith in the one God who has spoken to humanity through the prophets.[23] This monotheism is universal: surpassing the notion of a god for each people (henotheism), it recognizes a unique God, "creator of heaven and earth," offered to the recognition of all humans, in all times and in all places, even though this God may choose individuals (prophets) and a people (the believing community) to carry God's message to humanity.

In this context, the Qur'ān and Islam occupy a preeminent place in the collection of inquiries of all sorts, which the life of human beings unceasingly addresses to the Christian faith. Some of us would willingly include the Qur'ān in what the theology of non-Christian religions has termed "special revelation," a special moment in "general revelation" that gives it its meaning.[24] Others refer to the birth and development of the qur'anic revelation and the break experienced at Medina, which declared Islam to be a religion connected directly to Abraham and gathered to its bosom (according to its own perspective) elements from the other two religions. These persons would see the tie to Abraham more in terms of the attitude of faith in the one God as described in the Epistle to the Hebrews (11:8–19) and the Qur'ān (37:103); *islam* is the acceptance in faith of the mysterious order to sacrifice the son.[25] In either case, the monotheistic affirmation of the Muslim faith is a questioning of the Christian faith in God as one in three, and an exhortation to purify one's theological outlook and the forms of one's religious life. We shall say more of this when we discuss the consequences of the attitude we would adopt vis-à-vis the Qur'ān.

Another expression of the Word of God is that of a monotheism that is shared but different.

Before proceeding to this final stage of our reflection, it seems appropriate to recall that we are here (as in the foregoing paragraphs) developing *a Christian point of view*. This means two things. First, however far we have been able to carry it in the light of our Christian faith, we could never join this perspective to the essence of the Muslim faith, especially to its vision of the history of revelation, which culminates and terminates in the Qur'ān as the ultimate scripture manifesting the eternal Word of God, transmitted by Muhammad, "the seal of the prophets" (Qur'ān 33:40). Correlatively, there is no question of asking our Muslim partners to step into our specifically Christian perspectives, just as there can be no suggestion of finding in our thinking the totality and specificity of the Islamic idea of revelation. But on both sides we need to move our respective theologies forward, so that they may take the fullest account of what our experience has shown us about the faith of our partners, in complete respect for the essence of our own faith.

This said, our new approach has been foreshadowed by what we have said several times: there is no Word of God in the pure state. Even in special cases, in Jesus Christ according to Christians or in the Qur'ān accoring to Muslims, no revelation can claim to exhaust the mystery of God and the possibilities of communicating God's Word. Furthermore, because of the limitations and inadequacies of any communication in human language, we can never require a perfect accord in everything we acknowledge to be an expression of the Word of God. This is patently obvious between the Old and New Testament, and even within the New Testament. Why should we demand it elsewhere?

For this reason, the double loyalty to the Word we have received in Jesus Christ and to the Word our experience as Christians has led us to recognize in the Qur'ān, as well as our utter respect for all that these Words have in common and for their irreconcilable originality, all bring us to make this suggestion: to see the Qur'ān as an authentic Word of God, but one in part essentially different from the Word in Jesus Christ.

What our respective faiths have in common is especially and essentially the monotheism of the transcendent God. It has become almost a truism to say so, and we thank God for that; but it is not enough to rejoice in this mutual recognition, which still has a long way to go. It is necessary to set its authentic dimensions in order to avoid any possible distortions.

There is no need to insist on our rejection of a "common front" of monotheists against atheists or anyone at all. Believers are to witness to their faith and respect the freedom of everyone else.

There is a more subtle ambiguity in a union of monotheists in the same faith in the one God. Such a union would betray our respective faiths if it reduced them to a common denominator, because that would ask all believers to desert the specificity of their faith. Voices are sometimes heard to argue in this direction, but it would ruin our faiths to have them reduced to a notion of Oneness, however reasonable this might seem to philosophic principle: if God exists, there can only be one. This is the *De Deo uno* of our theodicies.

By way of contrast, a communion is fully legitimate as a faith in God *who is revealed to be unique.* This is a part of God's mystery revealed to us, and so this oneness remains mysterious. It is not reducible to arithmetic unity. In this basic movement of faith in the God who has been revealed as unique and in adherence to God's mystery, Christians and Muslims find themselves profoundly united, "brothers and sisters in faith."

This communion is an important point, but it is also important to add that Christian monotheism and Islamic monotheism are inherently different. A first divergence comes at the level of the culmination of revelation. For Christians, this is in Jesus Christ, the incarnate Word of God. For Muslims, it is in the Qur'ān, the ultimate revelation that recapitulates all others and is transmitted by the "seal of the prophets" (Qur'ān 33:40).

But the basis and justification of this first divergence should not be reduced to a question of chronology. The major divergence is to be found at the level of this very monotheism that we have said was held in common. More exactly, it is at the level of the transcendence of the one God. For the Qur'ān and Islam, the notion of creation links and at the same time radically separates the Creator and creatures (Surah 112). For the Christian faith, which with the Bible recognizes this radical cleavage, the Creator has taken the initiative of becoming a creature in Jesus Christ, true God and true human being.

The Qur'ān expresses its rejection of a God who would become human in the denial that Jesus could be anything but a servant and worshiper (ʿabd, Qur'ān 43:49), even though he was a very great prophet, miraculously born of the Virgin Mary. He is not a son (*ibn*) of God (9:30), for God has no child (*walad*) (19:34–35, 112). As a consequence, Jesus is not God (5:72, 116–117) and not the "third of a triad (of Gods)" (4:171; 5:73), for God is one, not three (4:171). Jesus said so himself (3:51; 19:30) and he repudiated those who took him and his mother to be gods (5:116–18).

As we have already observed, the doctrines denied by the Qur'ān are not genuine Christian doctrines. The incarnation and the divine sonship of Christ do not have the fleshly implication that the word *walad* (child) would suggest. The Trinity is not a triad of gods. Does this mean, as some have suggested, that the Qur'ān does not refer to these authentic Christian doctrines and even that it is not incompatible with them? The answer has come long ago from Muslim authors who well understood the Christian doctrines. Bīrūnī (11th century), who was aware of the metaphoric (we would say analogous) import of the terms "father" and "son," and the pseudo-Ghazāli of the *Radd Jamīl* (12th century), who saw these as particular "divine names" and accepted the doctrine of "persons" (*aqānīm*) within the Trinity, and all others concluded with the affirmation that Christian monotheism was incompatible with Islamic monotheism.

This is indeed so. Our faiths in God diverge over the conception of monotheism and even over the conception—or the approach—of God, before they come to express themselves in different dogmas. It is, furthermore, noteworthy that these "qur'anic *negations* of the Christian mysteries" are above all *affirmations* of Islamic monotheism. It is the latter that is at stake and not primarily the "Christian doctrines" or, even less, Jesus, that great prophet who could obviously not have said such things.

Even within a common faith in the revealed oneness of God, Islam emphasizes both an internal unbreakable oneness (this may be the meaning of the divine name *al-ṣamad*, Qur'ān 112:2: an unbreakable and impenetrable block) and the absolute transcendence of God the creator. Christianity believes in a differentiated oneness of God, which constitutes God's life and internal dynamism, leading God to bridge the abyss (the act of creation) that separates God from humanity and come to share its life by becoming, in the Son, a real human being. The God of Jesus Christ, of the Christian faith, is a God who in Jesus the incarnate Son is born, suffers, and dies before rising from the tomb.

Here, too, the approach to God is different in Islam and Christianity. The Islamic approach is primarily doctrinal[26] before it is soteriological.[27] The Qur'ān says that we must affirm God as being, as the unique and transcendent Being. Christianity follows the faith of Israel in Yahweh (Exod. 3:14), this God who bestows self-revelation by acting in the world, not primarily by declarations. Jesus takes up the Jewish notion of God the Father and gives it a new meaning: Father of all humans and no longer of one particular ethnic group, and he shows in his acts and words that he is the "Son" in a unique sense. The death and resurrection of Jesus, who has "entered into the glory of the Father," induced the early Christians to define God as love (1 John 4:8) revealed by the Son in the Spirit (a frequent formulation of St. Paul's). After the councils, theologians sought to translate this life of love within God as an exchange among the three divine persons: the Father loves the Son, the Son loves the Father, and the bond of love between them is the Spirit.

By definition and especially as exemplified by the life of Jesus, to love is to give oneself. In the heart of God, it is the gift and communion among the three Persons, whom it defines in their difference. In the relationship between God and creation, love is the gift of the Son, made human to reveal this love and to call other humans to live in it.

But this God incarnate never abandons unity and transcendence. God does not "mix" with humanity. Therein is the paradox, or rather the mystery, of the Christian faith. One can reject it or say it is impossible. One can question its formulation and its consequences. One cannot, however, deny the intention that is at the origin of the effort of reflection and underlies its development. It is significant that the long and subtle "christological" debates of the first Christian centuries, which would lead to the formulation of the dogmas of the Trinity and the incarnation, were finally to affirm that it was really God who became a human being in Jesus Christ. From this conclusion there followed the incarnation and the double nature of Christ in the Person of the Word, as well as the Trinity with the three Persons in a single divine nature. As one theologian said: "All christology is in the final analysis theo-logy," a teaching about God.

Nobody will deny that this approach to God is very different from that of Islam. Nevertheless, the Christian faith also intends to remain faithful to the oneness of God, against all polytheisms ancient and modern, and to God's transcendence against the various monisms and pantheisms. But its faithfulness is different from Islam's. In particular, the paradox—or, better, the mystery—of a God who becomes human without ceasing to be transcendent God is an invitation not to preset the limits of initiative for God, who "transcends" our human categories to be a "scandal to Jews and folly to gentiles" (1 Cor. 1:23).

But then, some may say, if these two concepts of monotheism, these two approaches to God, are different and irreconcilable, one is true and the other is false. One must choose, for God cannot "speak" several times in contradictory language. We have already sketched a preliminary response, setting these contradictions not in the order of the Word of God in God, but in the order of the human words that are necessary and inevitable for the Word of God to be extended to and received by humans in their own idiom.

The Christian faith in a triune God calls us further. If God is intrinsically an exchange of love, a communication, and a vision in the difference of the persons, God invites us to recognize and respect the difference between humans, between religions, and therefore between different versions of the Word of God.[28] A monolithic conception of the oneness of God would tend to project itself on human history and to spill into the absolute and exclusive. On the other hand, a respect for the mystery of God (both in the trinitarian formulation of Christianity and in Islam's mysterious oneness of God) demands a respect for every experience of God and God's Word in its differences from our own. Such differences, recognized and accepted, can be a source of mutual enrichment.

TOWARD A MUSLIM PERCEPTION OF THE BIBLE

Preliminary Remarks

1. It is important to begin a Muslim communication to a Muslim-Christian group with the declaration that a Muslim's point of view represents above all a personal opinion. It goes without saying that any "serious" opinion about religion presupposes a certain integration within the Islamic community. But it does not necessarily coincide with the prevailing consensus, for Islam has no magisterium to legitimate one opinion or another. Every seeker who fulfils certain basic conditions[29] can claim to read the

qur'anic text and Islamic tradition, and offer a personal viewpoint.

2. The "phenomenal ignorance" of the Christian world in general regarding the Qur'ān has its absolute counterpart in the phenomenal ignorance of the Muslim world about the text of the Bible. Awareness of the Bible remains limited to a few milieux and a few small groups. Where it occurs, it is often the result of fortuitous circumstances, like a meeting with missionaries, contacts with Christians living in Muslim countries, or life among Christians experienced by students or migrant workers. It can also be the result, but much less often, of intellectual curiosity or the requirements of religious apologetic in all its forms. This ignorance can be essentially explained on two different but complementary levels: Muslims were convinced, on the one hand, that the Qur'ān was sufficient, because it offered all the guarantees of authenticity and because it was the perfect revelation sent to fulfill all previous revelations and abrogate their laws; on the other hand, Islam had a religious monopoly on society, which reduced to a minimum any exchanges with non-Muslims, including Christians.

3. Today, we are watching the development of a phenomenon without precedent in the history of Muslim societies. These societies are starting to experience religious and, more generally, ideological pluralism. This varies of course from one country to another, and Islam still has a dominant position in those areas where it has long been solidly in place. But it has lost its immediate and evident character, as well as its capacity to constrain, in several important sectors of society and in an ever-increasing range of social classes. Day by day it is becoming more and more a matter of personal choice. This implies a conscious preference for Islam over other religions and, therefore, a modicum of information about them. As far as the Bible is concerned, the Qur'ān itself furnished this information. Hence the need to go back to this basic scriptural source and to the tradition of the Prophet, as well as the principal theological and exegetic tendencies that have characterized Muslim attitudes to the Bible.[30]

The Authorities: Scripture and Tradition

CONTACTS WITH ARABIAN CHRISTIANS

Today's Muslim-Christian dialogue has antecedents in the long and varied contact between the two communities, but we need not dwell on this here. Suffice it to say that information about the religious situation in Arabia at the dawn of Islam is very rudimentary. It is nevertheless certain that there were polytheists, Jews, and Christians on the scene.

The Christian community in Hijaz, the cradle of Islam, seems to have been less structured than the Jewish groups. Christians lived mostly in the frontier areas (the Manadhira of Hirah, vassals of the Persians, were Nestorians; the Ghassanis of Syria, vassals of Byzantium, were Monophysites, as, probably, were the Najran in Yemen), which did not come under Islamic control until after the death of the Prophet. As for the Jews, they occupied centers of much more strategic importance, like Medina and Khaybar, and they quickly came into conflict with nascent Islam. When the Qur'ān speaks of "people of the book" (*ahl al-kitāb*) in general, it usually refers to the Jews.

In the early days of Islam there was a favorable prejudice regarding Christians, especially the religious among them:

> We gave him (Jesus) the Gospel and set in the hearts of those who followed him mercy and compassion. They invented monasticism—we did not prescribe it for them—only seeking God's pleasure. But they did not observe it as they ought to have. We gave to those who believed among them their reward, but many of them are sinners [Qur'ān 57:27].

Elsewhere, Christians were accused of a certain "deviation"; but relations between them and Muslims were cordial. Muslims had even found refuge in the domains of the Negus of Ethiopia. There were some disagreements of course, especially with the Christians of Najran,[31] but nothing like the extremely strained relations between the first Muslims and the Jews. We should also remark that when the Qur'ān speaks of *nasārā* (Christians), it refers to those who adhere more or less to the oriental churches and consider themselves to be adepts of Christianity.

TAḤRĪF

The Qur'ān often refers to the scriptures of the "people of the book," accusing them of *tahrīf*. This term has generally been translated, in a somewhat exaggerated way, by "alteration," "falsification." In fact, it is simply a question of deviation, which can take a variety of forms.[32]

Let us remember Mohammed Talbi's fine expression: "Tahrif is the deviation suffered by the divine ray when it passes through the deforming prism of our imperfect humanity."[33]

The study of qur'anic vocabulary concerning *tahrīf* reveals the following concepts:

Tahrīf: Qur'ān 2:75; 4:46; 5:13; 5:41.

Tabdīl (substitution): 2:59; 7:162.

Kitmān (the act of hiding or concealing words or passages of scripture so that the Muslims would not know about them): 2:42, 140, 146, 159, 174; 3:71, 187.

Labs (clothing, disguising): 2:42; 3:71.

Layy ("twisting" the tongue in the mouth while reading the scripture, so that the hearer does not understand, or understands something else): 3:78; 4:46.

Nisyān (forgetting part of the scripture): 5:13, 14; 7:53, 165.[34]

From such qur'anic references, Muslim authors who have studied this problem of *tahrīf* have elaborated three forms of falsification:

1. A falsification of *the text (taḥrīf al-naṣṣ)*: for example, Ibn Hazm (d. 428/1063): stories about the choice of the first Apostles, the resurrection of Jairus's daughter; Juwaini (d. 478/1085): on the genealogies of Jesus, Peter's threefold denial, the triumphal entry into Jerusalem, the crucifixion and death of Jesus.

2. Falsification of *the meaning (taḥrīf al-ma'ānī)*: Avicenna (d. 428/1037), Ghazālī (505/1111), Ibn Khaldun (808/1406), Muhammad 'Abduh (1321/1905).

3. A new conception of *taḥrīf,* based on the more or less clear perception of the difference between the Christian idea of inspiration and the Muslim idea of revelation. Without tarrying over the details of this question, let us add a few brief remarks.

As we shall see, the qur'anic passages about *taḥrīf* go beyond the verses where these key words are to be found.

In nearly all these verses, *taḥrīf* is ascribed to the Jews rather than the Christians. There are allusions to actual events in Medinese life, so these are not absolute judgments.

It is true that Christianity subsumes the Old Testament. But we must not forget that the Muslim perspective is always directed to the notion of the "book." The Jewish and Christian communities belong to the "people of the book": the Jews are the adherents of the Torah and the Christians are the followers of the Gospel.

In the Qur'ān, *ahl al-kitāb* means first and foremost the Jews, and only indirectly the Christians. But later tradition, which was generally popularizing and careless of the details of the "circumstances of revelation" *(asbāb al-nuzūl)*, applied these judgments to the two religions without distinction, and even came, in response to the vagaries of history, to apply them more to Christians than to Jews.

We glean little about Christianity from these theories. We must therefore *work from concrete examples*, where the Qur'ān addresses Christians in particular and accuses them of a specific *taḥrīf.* We prefer to work from the qur'anic text itself, putting between parentheses—as far as possible—the influence of the later "ideological stock," but always bearing in mind that the Qur'ān also responds to a given historical and sociological situation.

THE MAJOR THEMES OF CHRISTIAN TAḤRĪF ACCORDING TO THE QUR'ĀN

Jesus, the Son of God

The Qur'ān insists on the fact that Jesus is a prophet and the son of Mary, not the son of God (see 61:6; 9:30; 72:3; 112:3). These affirmations have their corollaries in the utter denial of *divinity in Jesus,* the rejection of an *exaggerated veneration of Mary,* which would make her not just the mother of Jesus but the mother of God, and, obviously, the rejection of the doctrine of the Trinity, which is considered to be a type of unacceptable partnership.

The exegetes reported that, according to the *asbab al-nuzul,* a Jew and a Christian from Najran said to the Prophet: "Do you want to be worshiped?"

"God forbid," he replied. "Only God should be worshiped."

Then the following verse was revealed:

> It is not possible for any human to whom God has given the book, and wisdom, and the gift of prophecy to say to people: "Be my worshipers instead of God's." No! Be masters of what you have learned and studied in the book [Qur'ān 3:79; cf. 43:49].

Several other verses point in the same direction:

> God said: O Jesus son of Mary! Did you say to the people: "Take me and my mother as gods apart from God?" Jesus replied: "Glory to You! It was not for me to say what I have no right to say. You would have known if I had said this!" [5:116].

> They are unbelievers who say: "God is the Messiah Son of Mary." The Messiah himself said: "Children of Israel, worship God, my Lord and your Lord! To whoever ascribes partners to God, God denies entry into paradise, and that person's abode will be the fire [5:72; cf. 5:17].

> The Messiah son of Mary was only a messenger, other messengers had preceded him. His mother was a saint. They both ate food. See how we make clear to them the signs and see how they turn away [5:75].

> They are surely unbelievers who say that God is the third of three. There is only the one God. If they do not desist from saying this, a painful affliction will strike unbelievers [5:73].

> Believe in God and God's messengers and do not say "Three" [4:171].

We should first of all note that the Qur'ān takes the expression "son of God" literally. It repudiates a human conception through carnal relations between God and Mary. It is doubtless in this naive manner that the Christian Arabs of the early seventh century, particularly in the poorer classes, understood the matter; and the average Muslim of today is not far from sharing the same idea. To what extent can contemporary Christians recognize themselves in these affirmations that the Qur'ān attributes to the Christians of its time?

We believe that Islam could tolerate any metaphorical interpretation that distanced itself from this basic sense. Perhaps some theologians would disapprove of such an expression because of the risk of ambiguity, following the well-known principle of the barrier of expedients (*sadd al-dharā'i'*).[35] But it remains true that the Muslim faith categorically rejects the idea that Jesus could really be the son of God, eternally begotten of the Father in the bosom of the Trinity. The God of Muslim faith is not a God to be born and to die like the Christian deity. For Muslims, God's transcendence is absolute.

Even though he was a human, Jesus was certainly not like other humans. He was born without a father; this was his principal miracle. In the Qur'ān this birth is compared to the creation of Adam, who had neither mother nor father, to show the divine omnipotence. But Adam's case is in fact easier to understand, for it is the beginning of a sequence, whereas Jesus represents a break in a well-established sequence. According to the Qur'ān itself, Jesus is "a word coming from God" (3:39, 45; 4:171; 5:170). The Word of God for most Muslims is an eternal attribute of God. In the creation of Jesus, there was a *divine intervention* more evident than in the rest of creation: "We breathed into her [Mary] of Our Spirit" (21:91; 66:12). In Jesus there is a *divine aspect* superior to the aspect that exists in every human being as an heir to the first divine creation in the image of God by which humanity became God's lieutenant on earth. Jesus is a revelation, a miracle, a manifestation of God, but not God. "We made of her [Mary] and her son a sign (*āya*) for all peoples" (21:91; 23:50).

The Crucifixion

The crucifixion of Jesus is a major point in Christian belief. What does the Qur'ān say about it? We think that Muslims deny Jesus' death and especially his crucifixion, quoting the verse: "They neither killed nor crucified him" (4:157). In order to understand this verse, we must set it in its qur'anic and historical context. This is a context of polemic against the Jews of Medina: "And [we cursed them] because of their unbelief and their egregious calumny against Mary and their having said, 'We killed the Messiah Jesus son of Mary, the messenger of God,' *when they neither killed nor crucified him*, but it *only appeared so to them*" (4:156–58).

As we see it, we have here a vehement retort against Jews who were congratulating themselves for having killed Jesus. Is it possible to see in the qur'anic response an image that would signify that, even if they killed and crucified him, they could never overcome the ideals he preached?

In any case, there are other verses that allude to the *death of Jesus*:

God said, "Jesus, I shall cause you to die and I shall take you up to me; I shall deliver you from the unbelievers. I shall set those who have followed you above those who have not believed, until the day of resurrection" (3:55).

When you took me up to you (*tawaffayta-nī*), you are the one who watched over them. You are the witness of everything" (5:117).

They are unbelievers indeed who have said: "God is the Messiah, the son of Mary." Say: "Whoever can in any way overrule God, if God chooses to exterminate (*yuhlika*) the Messiah, son of Mary and his mother, and everyone on earth?" (5:17).

"Peace be upon me [Jesus] the day I was born and *the day I die* and the day I am raised alive" (19:33).

These verses have bothered some exegetes who could not avoid advancing *the hypothesis of the death of Jesus* before his ascension.[36] Others have relegated this death to the end of time. There have also been some Christians who believed that Jesus' sufferings were only apparent.[37] But the two religions consider that the end of Jesus' life on earth was "extra-ordinary" and that God took him up, whether after his death and resurrection (for Christians) or without death or crucifixion (for Muslims). In such a situation the crucifixion would also be merely appearance. The divine intervention served to confuse the adversaries at that time. But the mystery still remains and nobody should claim to have resolved it categorically. Our two traditions, Christian and Muslim, agree on the historical failure of the prophet Jesus and, in very different ways, on the divine intervention that followed this failure by raising Jesus to heaven, with or without a death on the cross, according to Islamic tradition, and by raising him to life after his death, according to Christian tradition.

The Proclamation of Muhammad's Prophethood

In Islam, the prophets belong to one family. They proclaim and recognize one another, and they contribute, each as well as possible, to the realization of the divine plan:

> When God made a covenant with the prophets [God said]: "Behold what I give you of Book and wisdom. One day a prophet will come affirming what you have. Believe in him and help him." God said: "Do you agree and do you accept My covenant on that condition?" They answered: "We agree." God said: "So bear witness. I shall be a witness with you" [3:81].

Abraham, the father of the three monotheist religions, proclaimed the prophethood of Muhammad (2:129) and Muhammad's name was written in the Torah and the gospel:

> The *ummi* [illiterate? gentile?] prophet whom they will find mentioned in the Torah and the Gospel [7:157].

> "I am the messenger of God," said Jesus son of Mary to his people. "I come to confirm the Torah that was before me and to announce to you that a messenger will come after me, and his name will be Aḥmad" [61:6].

This point has been considered fundamental in the relationship of Islam to Christianity (Qur'ān 5:68). For obvious reasons, it is hard for Christianity to accept this. Its position can be compared to that of Judaism with regard to both Christianity and Islam. The problem does not confront Islam in the same terms, given that it is the last monotheistic religion in chronological order and it can easily recognize the earlier religions. As for Muslim thinkers, they have throughout history taken great pains to scour the Jewish and Christian scriptures for passages that could support this assertion. They have not failed to find some, especially those that refer to the sending of the Paraclete.[38]

What can we conclude after this hasty enumeration of the main points of *tahrīf* according to the Qur'ān?

None of the fundamental points of divergence between Islam and Christianity has been unknown within Christendom, before and after the appearance of Islam. Theories akin to the Islamic notions and foreign to the official doctrine of the church and its mysteries have existed at all times in Christian thought.[39] However, they represent rather marginal tendencies.

The Islamic interpretation of these passages has not always been as rigid as one may suppose. It has simply been dominated by a polemic and combative ideology that consistently stressed the divergences.

The long discussions of these points, in both Islam and Christianity, show that they are the basic points of theology, of the relationship between God and the human being and human destiny, in which the divine mystery has an eminent place and where the human spirit is not entitled to propose rigid solutions that would reduce the content of the Word of God.

Muslim apologetic starts from a false analogy between the ideas of revelation and inspiration. A dialogue of the deaf has resulted from this misunderstanding. It should also be said that the classic Christian viewpoint, which was too closely bound to the letter of the sacred text, did nothing to help Muslim apologetic to evolve. We think that the Muslim theory of *tah rīf* could now be fully congruent with the textual criticism of the Bible as Christians have developed it.

In our understanding of Islam and Christianity, we think that *tahrīf* is not as basic as is generally thought, but it is very important to start with the qur'anic text itself and set it carefully in its historical and sociological context. There should be no question of stubbornly digging for contradictions in the Christian scriptures in order to unmask *tahrīf*.

Christianity (and one could also say Judaism) is a component of Islam, just as Judaism is a component of Christianity.[40] It represents a way of truth, as is evident for the pre-Islamic era. For the post-Islamic period, Muslim thinkers have not agreed on "the salvation of *ahl al-kitāb*," probably because of the degree of *tahrīf* of which they are accused. Many of these thinkers believe that the "abode of reward" will be open to sincere non-Muslims of good faith.[41] Islamic tradition insists that the only unpardonable sin is *shirk* (ascribing partners to God). Sunnis even think that final judgment is in the hands of God, who can do anything. Contrary to the teaching of the Mu'tazilis, God is not bound to respect any particular logic in applying threats and promises.

Another point seems basic to us, and Muslims must accept it: there can

be no conscious *taḥrīf;* to undermine one's own faith is the very denial of
faith, unless one posits the existence of an evil genius that duped all Christians.

During the centuries after the spread of Islam, Muslim theologians discussed with relative equanimity the salvation of a person living in isolation
who could have no awareness of Islam.

It is said that this hypothesis would be difficult to imagine in our own
times. Perhaps. But it would be a serious mistake to think that the obvious
facility of communication has proportionally improved familiarity with the
other. It would be wise to be a little less confident regarding the evidence
for "our truth"; most of it is inherited. There is, besides, a *hadith* to the
effect that the human being is born according to the *fiṭra,* and it is the
parents who make the child a Jew or a Christian.[42] This conditioning by
the geographic and historical environment is very real and must be considered as an "attenuating circumstance" in the human person's difficult
search for truth. It should therefore inspire in us greater modesty, greater
tolerance, and a recognition of the right to be different. This difference
seems part of God's will:

> If God had so willed, God would have made of you one community.
> But God would test you as you are. So vie with one another in good
> works. You will all return to God, who will tell you about the object
> of your divergences [Qur'ān 5:48].

Our Suggestions

This glimpse of Muslim tradition shows that the phenomenon of Jewish-
Christian revelation is often present in Muslim reflection, even outside the
specifically polemic tradition. There is a difference with Christianity, which
seeks to determine the status of a revelation that came after the Jesus
Christ event, whereas for Islam the status of the Bible was established from
the advent of the Qur'ān: it is a revelation for Jews and Christians,
superseded by the qur'anic revelation addressed to all humanity.

This reflection leads us to two important conclusions:

1. There is no difficulty in recognizing that God spoke to humans before
Muhammad. On the contrary, it is an act of faith to accept the revelations
given to earlier prophets, especially Jesus.

2. The Bible has a privileged status among the sacred books other than
the Qur'ān; one thinks of the books of the Mazdeans, the Manicheans, the
Sabeans. However, the Qur'ān remains the ultimate revelation and the
criterion of truth, even though it does not include everything that God
could reveal to humans (Qur'ān 18:109 and 31:27).

Muslims, therefore, have no problem recognizing Christian scripture as
a Word of God. Beyond this principle, it remains to be seen whether or
not the various books that comprise the Bible are in conformity with the

messages transmitted by the prophets, and in particular whether or not the Gospels of the New Testament correspond to the gospel of Jesus, his message in words and actions.

Indeed, the New Testament is made up of the four Gospels of Matthew, Mark, Luke, and John, the Acts of the Apostles, the Epistles, and the Apocalypse. So it is not limited to the message of Jesus. The New Testament contains the interpretation of Jesus' message made by the first generations of Christians; his own words are embedded in the matrix of apostolic witness.

Is it possible, then, from a Muslim point of view, to recognize the New Testament as an expression of the Word of God? Yes and no. Yes, to the extent that it contains the marks of the divine message transmitted by Jesus to the Jews, although it would be difficult to distinguish with any certainty between what Jesus really said and what he did not say. No, to the extent that if we do not accept the idea that the Holy Spirit inspired the authors of the New Testament, it is a human composition lacking the authority of the Messenger. Anything derived from the testimony of Jesus' contemporaries or the traditions formed about him cannot be considered the Word of God.

It could be said that the principal criterion of authenticity for a non-Muslim revelation, and for Christian revelation in particular, is not so much its conformity or noncontradiction with the Qur'ān as the faithfulness of its transmission from the prophet-messenger.

Whether we understand *taḥrīf* as a corruption of the text or a bad interpretation, the question only refers us to this distance between the revealed message of Jesus and its textual objectification. This is all the more true as the New Testament is the expression of a notion of the oneness and transcendence of God that is apparently incompatible with the qur'anic conception.

Such as it is, however, the Christian scripture can be of interest to Muslims. They can find in it an emphasis on certain values that are certainly not absent from the Qur'ān, but are insufficiently cultivated in Muslim circles, like love, forgiveness, the rejection of pharisaism, and the concern with the spirit rather than the letter of the law. Moreover, and even as they bear in mind the difference in the mode of revelation between the Muslim and Christian scriptures, Muslims must be wary of harping on this difference and learn to ponder what the Bible says about the source of life, which can nourish the believer's hope and spirituality.

We think that beyond the negative attitude that sees the authors of the New Testament as impostors who consciously falsified and corrupted Jesus' message, there are several other possible attitudes. These are not mutually exclusive:

1. An attitude of waiting. We have before us two scriptures, one presenting itself as the work of persons who testify to their faith in Christ risen and alive, and the other as the divine message of which the Prophet is but

the faithful transmitter. In this case, we must "live the contradiction without being able to surmount it with a broader perspective."

2. A doctrinal attitude. We could recognize the New Testament—and particularly the Gospels—as an authentic Word of God, but mixed with human interventions, which are not solely concerned with the passage of the ineffable Word of God to its expression in the human language of the prophet. The impossibility of separating these two elements, divine and human, is the principal obstacle to giving the Bible the same status as the Qur'ān.

3. These two attitudes, which we have observed among a great many Muslims, do not satisfy us. It seems possible to go still further, on both doctrinal and existential planes.

On *the doctrinal plane*, we believe that Muslims, like Christians, are called to determine the precise status of the "authorized" interpretive testimony offered by the New Testament. Considered solely in terms of its faithfulness to the message of Jesus—that is, to his gospel—this becomes a field of research open to critical inquiry and analysis. This would in fact be a question of trying to establish the measure of the New Testament's internal cohesion compared to its objective, which is to express in experiential terms what Jesus wanted to say in claiming to help his disciples to know the will of the one who had sent him. There is here an examination that does not necessarily build on historico-critical analysis but could nevertheless lead to a common elaboration of a new notion of the message.

On *the existential plane*, the accent should be on the effect of the text that Christians have considered canonical on the life and conscience of those who live by it, rather than the way in which it was produced.

We would thus be obliged to recognize that this text is for them a privileged access to faith in the one God, the God of Abraham, Isaac, and Jacob, Moses, Jesus, and Muhammad. God is revealed to them through its mediation. It is worthy of Muslim respect, for it is a way that leads to God and love for one's neighbor, which is the main thing in the view of Islam. This way certainly differs from the path of Islam in many respects; it is not the best way, in the judgment of Islam. But we ought not to put ourselves in God's place and decide whether to reject or disqualify it.

In this perspective, we prefer not to tamper with the—loaded—concept of the Word of God. We say so not only because the Word of God in Christian terms is the Christ, but also because any formal recognition would be much less important than an open approach that encouraged us to "present ourselves before God with a pure heart" (Qur'ān 26:89).

Conclusion

As we have already said, the suggestions we have put forward are in no way intended to give general and definitive solutions to the serious problems that scripture poses to Christian and Muslim believers today. Besides, the foregoing text, which is the fruit of the group's work over five years, is only the tip of an "iceberg" whose submerged base is composed of the individual contributions of the members and the discussions at local sessions and in the general assemblies. All these had a rather abundant richness,[1] bringing to light the complexity of the problems, offering explanations for historical or static attitudes, clarifying or unsettling established positions, suggesting avenues of research and leaving doors open.

With a common accord, we have preferred to leave these doors open. We have confidence in reflection about religious material that we know to be in a full process of evolution in both our communities, despite phases of intransigence, which are local and—we firmly hope—transitory. It is our world itself that is evolving and forever discovering "new territories." A religion enclosed in the schemes of the past would sooner or later be invalidated.

We are not unaware of the risks involved in new interpretations of our religious heritage. But life is full of risks. Only death has ultimate assurance. That is why we have put *questions*, rather than solutions, for the reflection of our religions. We wish now to restate them here, as a form of conclusion.

1. If it is agreed that the Word of God reaches humans in a human language set in time—which in no way alters faith in its truth—what consequences should be drawn for our interpretation of the scriptures? For example, to what extent must the information given by one scripture about another, or about the faith of another set of beliefs, be taken literally or reset in the context of time and place?

More generally, is the goal of our scriptures the delivery of historical information or the suggestion through historical examples of religious values that transcend time? If metaphorical language seems to be the least inadequate for expressing the mystery of God and God's relationship with humanity, how are we to understand metaphors like the Word of God,[2] scripture, Son of God? And if we concede that no human language can adequately and integrally express the Word of God, how can we understand the passages of our respective scriptures that seem to present these scriptures as perfect and complete? Moreover, if the corpus of our scriptures is closed, how can we draw from it the inexhaustible implications that it conceals, but which are required by the challenges of our own age?

2. When believers in one religion seek to understand the faith of believers in another religion, they must necessarily go back to the terms of their own faith: they "reread their own scripture." But what are the *criteria* that could guide this rereading? One's experience of the authenticity of the partner's faith? The "openings" allowed by one's own founding text? The elaborations of one's tradition?

In other words, the crucial problem is to combine faithfulness without concessions to the essence of the message of our scriptures with the broadest recognition of the cogency of our partner's faith. But what is the criterion for distinguishing between the essential and the accidental in the text of scripture?

3. In the course of our work, we have frequently remarked that the *theologies* elaborated over time in both our traditions were heavily dependent on their particular historical contexts. As these traditions have lived to a great extent in isolation (until very recently), these theologies were themselves usually "theologies of exclusion," engineered to shut the doors our scriptures could have opened. For example, with regard to the *taḥrīf* (alteration) of prequr'anic scriptures, we noted that the relevant point of inclusion in the Qur'ān was narrow and very circumstantial, and the idea had later been inflated into a key concept for explaining the anterior scriptures. We made a similar observation with regard to the "closing of scripture" in the Christian tradition, which, torn from the context in which it had been formulated, falsely acquired the meaning of a general closing of revelation.

This is especially so in the case of the "theologies of revelation" elaborated on one side and the other. It is clear that these theologies took only one scriptural phenomenon into account: the Bible for Christian theology, the Qur'ān for Islamic theology. On the basis of this unique phenomenon, a general theory was constructed and then applied more or less appropriately to similar phenomena. Has the hour not come to reexamine these unilateral theologies? One of our number has spoken of a "deconstruction of orthodoxies." Would it not be necessary from now on to consider the whole set of phenomena of revelation in their diversity and their originality in order to design a theology of revelation that would be equally acceptable to a Jew, a Christian, and a Muslim, or that would at least give their scripture an undistorted image that everyone could recognize?

This applies to all aspects of theology. Is it conceivable, for example, that a Christian theologian would speak of faith without speaking of Muslim faith? Of revelation, without mentioning the Qur'ān? Of the Trinity or the incarnation without noting the reservation of Muslim faith? Similarly, is it conceivable that a Muslim theology would speak of the Torah or the Gospels without looking at these texts, or of Jesus without considering the thinking of Christians?

In this regard our respective thinkers or theologies seem too frequently to suffer from a major deficiency: that of freezing the thought of the other community in a stage that is past, or at least becoming so, under the term "classical theology" or "majority thinking," and ignoring current efforts at renewal. The very concept of "orthodoxy" is at least relative. Of course, we must not sacralize the latest opinion in its turn. But history has shown that new ideas, even if they are sometimes condemned, often turn out to be the most productive. Without anticipating the future, it is appropriate to take account of the life and the quests of our contemporary communities. This is indeed a difficult task, but is it not the work of researchers, who will be able to enlighten their colleagues?

4. A number of factors and agents shape the religious conscience, from the religious instruction of children to adult courses, from the training of future specialists in religion to literature and the latest means of communication, and we ask whether it is not time to marshal all these for a concerted recognition of the others in their originality and their authenticity. We have referred several times to the "phenomenal ignorance" of each of our religious communities regarding the other. In our exchanges, some of us have gone further, to speak not only of ignorance but of misappreciation, not only of a lack of information but also of deformation or, in today's terms, systematic disinformation.

Considerable work remains to be done at every level and in all areas in order that each person might have and present a vision of the other believer, which this other could recognize. This is the first stage, or at least an essential stage, in what we now call interfaith dialogue. We have experienced its productivity in the course of our work and it is without doubt the aspect that remains the most precious, whatever happens. This, finally, is our group's profound desire: to contribute to a more faithful and more respectful awareness of our respective religious traditions in order to help our coreligionists to live in harmony in a plural world.

5. To recognize each other in truth does not seem to be enough. If we believe that God acts within various religious traditions, then God also "speaks" to us through them and we must receive the challenge addressed to us by another faith, not only in what it may have in common with ours, but perhaps even more in what it has that is *different* and irreconcilable.

In this way, the intransigent affirmation of the oneness and transcendence of God in the Qur'ān and Muslim tradition could well warn the Christian against the deformation of — or at least an oversimplistic approach to — Christian doctrine and practice. This affirmation is certainly in line with the Old Testament where the Christians, and Jesus first of all, find their roots. But its proclamation today by hundreds of millions of Muslims, who are partners of Christians in so many fields, gives it a particular intensity. It invites the Christians to rediscover what is really essential to the revelation in Jesus Christ, at a time when this essence is often drowned in a vague deism derived more from religious sentiment than faith. It can also warn Christians against an absolutization of mediations. Faith in the God of Jesus Christ does not stop with the formulation of dogmas nor even, we daresay, with Christ himself. By rediscovering the very soul of Jesus, always turned toward the Father, and the soul of the liturgy (to the Father, through the Son, in the Spirit), it will turn like a magnet toward the God who is mysteriously one, transcendent, and present. As the theologians say, the last word about God is one of Unity, which, if we may refer to God in spatial images, is not nearer than the Trinity, but at the apex of its realization.

In a similar way, it would seem possible to think that Christian faith in the triune God could urge Muslims to respect the very mystery of this divine oneness, which cannot be reduced to a mathematical symbol or a rational deduction, by keeping or recapturing that sense of the mystery of God that is so vivid in the Qur'ān and has been so profoundly experienced by Muslim spirituality. At least, the testimonies of contemporary Muslims would seem to suggest this.

As well, the link that Duquoc has indicated between the difference in God to which the doctrine of the Trinity attests and a respect for the differences among humans, including religious differences, could alert us to the danger—so often decried, but not always observable in history—of linking a monolithic conception of monotheism with its projection in constrictive or totalitarian societies.

In this way the Christians' effort to accept, in truth and without condescension, the Word of God spoken in the Qur'ān, and the parallel—and common—effort of Muslims regarding the Bible, could dissolve many of the hypotheses that encumber the encounter between Christians and Muslims, their collaboration in the service of humanity, and their awareness of being truly brothers and sisters in faith in the one God. Every deepening of our common faith opens each of us to a recognition of the other. But this deepening is born, at least for us, of this very recognition, which is sometimes painful but always enriching.

At the end of this work on scripture, and so on the Word of God, it seems to us important to remember that God has also been manifested to humans in history through individual and collective experiences, inviting them to live the experience in God. Do our encounter and our common search not constitute a sign bringing a call to our times?

Appendixes

Here is the list of those who have contributed to the preparation of this volume, whether only in the local sections (Algeria, Beirut, Brussels, Paris, Rabat, Tunis) or during the annual meetings as well; in this latter case, the Roman numerals after certain names indicate the annual meetings in which they participated:

I Sénanque 1978
II Tunis 1979
III Sénanque 1980
IV Rabat 1981
V Tunis-Korbous 1982

The posts indicated for each name are those held during the period of our work (1977–1982).

ARKOUN, Mohammed, historian of Islamic thought, University of Paris II (I,II,III,IV,V).

BENJELLOUN-TOUIMI, Mohammed, professor of Arabic literature, Rabat (II,III,IV,V).

BLONDEL, Anne-Marie, Inspector of secondary education, Ministry of National Education, Tunis (II,V).

BOU-IMAJDIL, Abdesalam, professor of philosophy, Faculty of Arts and Social Sciences, Rabat (I,II,III,IV,V).

CASPAR, Robert, professor of Islamic theology, Monastir (Tunisia) and Rome (I,II,III,IV,V).

CHARFI, Abdelmajid, professor of Islamic studies, Faculty of Arts and Social Sciences, Tunis (I,II,III,IV,V).

CHEVRELIÈRE, Monique de la, linguist, Tunis (V).

CORBON, Jean, biblical scholar, Beirut.

CUOQ, Joseph, professor of history and Islamic studies, Tunis and Paris.

EYT, Pierre, rector of the Catholic Institute of Toulouse (I,II).

GABUS, Jean-Paul, theologian, Protestant Faculty, Brussels (II,III,IV,V).

GEFFRÉ, Claude, theologian, Catholic Institute of Paris (I,II,III,IV,V).

GELOT, Joseph, theologian, Tunis.

GHRAB, Saad, professor of Islamic studies, Faculty of Arts and Social Sciences, Tunis (I,II,III,V).

GUELLOUZ, Ezzeddine, librarian, National Library, Tunis (I).

HADDAD, Fatma, professor of philosophy, Faculty of Arts and Social Sciences, Tunis (II,V).

KHODR, Georges, Greek Orthodox archbishop of Mount Lebanon, Broummana, Lebanon (IV).

LAMBERT, Jean, professor of philosophy, Rabat (III,IV).

LAMBERT, Marie-Geneviève, professor of literature, Rabat (III,IV).

LANGHADE, Jacques, professor of Islamic studies, Faculty of Arts and Social Sciences, Rabat.

LELONG, Michel, professor at the Catholic Institute of Paris (I,II,III,IV,V).

LÉVRAT, Jacques, theologian, Rabat (I,II,III,IV,V).

MENSIA, Moqdad, professor of Islamic mysticism, Faculty of Theology, Tunis (V).

MONBARON, Jacqueline, professor of French, Rabat (IV).

MONBARON, Michel, geologist, Rabat (IV).

OFFRET, Jean Bosco, student of Islam, Rabat (IV).

RAHMATOULLAH, economist and student of Islam, Paris (III,IV).

REKIK, Kémal, polytechnic engineer, STEG, Tunis (V).

SAROCCHI, Jean, professor of French literature, Faculty of Arts and Social Sciences, Tunis.

SEGHROUCHNI, Driss, professor of Arabic literature, Rabat (III,IV).

SMITH-FLORENTIN, Françoise, professor of exegesis and biblical theology, Protestant Faculty of Paris (II,III,IV,V).

SPEIGHT, Marston, Methodist pastor and student of Islam, Tunis.

TALBI, Mohammed, professor of history, Faculty of Arts and Social Sciences, Tunis (II,V).

TAYLOR, John, director of the Department of Dialogue with People of Living Faiths and Ideologies, World Council of Churches, Geneva (I,III,IV).

VERGOTE, Henri-Bernard, professor of philosophy, Faculty of Arts and Social Sciences, Tunis.

ZNIBER, Mohammed, professor of history, Rabat (II,III,IV).

APPENDIX 2: RESERVATIONS

Before signing our text, two of our members wished to make the following reservations, which we reproduce in extenso, just as they were submitted to us.

Jean-Paul Gabus, Brussels

I am extremely happy to be able to sign this first collective work of GRIC, by means of which we have so greatly enriched one another.

I would nevertheless like to express two reservations and a final remark.

1. My first observation concerns the expression "the sense of the scripture" (p. 39). I believe that this expression directly contradicts what we previously decided: "The texts are bearers of a plural truth. The scripture is an abundance, not a unique system." It also contradicts all the observations we made concerning the fact that *every new reading creates meaning* and the whole of chapter 3: readings of the book. Finally, the last sentence of chapter 2: "The act of believing is a decision that finds a real meaning based on a tradition and a divergence with a drawing away from it with a view to a re-creation."

All we are saying tends to show that the meaning of a text is always the effect of a meeting between the reader and the text. The text, even though it is revealed, never bears the meaning, understood in our respective theological traditions to be desired or proposed by God. The meaning results from a linguistic and hermeneutic process. It is never deposited or inscribed in the text in advance.

This disparity in our language reappears in chapter 3 when we speak of the *meaning of the message*. It shows that we had a lot of trouble breaking the traditional mental habit fashioned by centuries of dogmatism and a fetishistic conception of meaning.

2. As a Reformed theologian, I do not feel at all at ease with the methodology proposed in the section of chapter 3 entitled "Toward a Christian Perception of the Qur'ān." Of course, I subscribe completely to the two criteria of judgment proposed for an appreciation of the authenticity (or lack thereof) of a nonbiblical revelation: *the content of the message and the productivity of this message.*

What bothers me is that the whole discussion is centered on *the oneness of the transcendent God*. I do not think that this point is as central and decisive as our document affirms. It seems to me that the biblical message is itself not uniquely focused on this problem, but on other points no less essential in my opinion, such as the relationship of God to human history, God's plan for the salvation and re-creation of the whole universe, the teaching of Jesus, his victory on the cross, and at his resurrection over the powers of sin and evil, the necessity of a conversion or new birth, made possible by an outpouring-inpouring of the Spirit in the heart of a believer in Jesus Christ. The qur'anic message seems to me scarcely to touch any of these themes, so important to the Christian church and our Christian praxis. I do not perceive the qur'anic revelation as simply different from the biblical revelation: I perceive it as incomplete in certain aspects, as I perceive the biblical revelation to be incomplete in other ways.

I am also troubled by the status accorded to the biblical text in chapter 3. The Bible is presented to us as the product of a religious history, that of the Jewish people, then the early Christian community. It seems to me that it would have been good to recall first of all that this text remains for the Christian community, even when it is seen from the angle of redaction history, a *text inspired* by God, and therefore normative. And whatever the subsequent theological tradition or the astonishing and encouraging opening of contemporary theological reflection could say will never relativize this normativity of the biblical text, or even less cause us to forget it.

3. Our conclusion underlines the exclusivism that has so far characterized our respective theological traditions and today's need to open ourselves to a recognition of other believers in their difference, and to whatever this difference may bring to challenge our own faith.

I accept this decision one hundred percent. But it seems to me that an immense theological effort remains for GRIC to undertake in this field. We have doubtless opened a few new avenues of research, and even possible consensus on important points of our faith. But on other points, we affirm that our positions remain irreconcilable and we do not go beyond the traditional bones of contention: Trinity, divinity of Christ, the meaning of his death on the cross, the nonnormative character of the other's scripture.

Without a doubt, we formulate these divergences in a less polemic and more open manner. But we have in no way overcome them.

It seems to me that we should question ourselves more deeply on *the reasons for our exclusivism*, which persists even when we pretend to say the contrary.

I wonder whether this abiding exclusivism does not have its source somewhere other than in the simply historical and contingent circumstances of nature; perhaps in the fact that Christian faith like Muslim faith claims to be the bearer of a *universality*. Precisely, is this universalism, of which our respective messages are the bearers, really compatible with this *authentic recognition of others in their differences*?

Up to the present, it seems to me that we have not believed this compatibility to be possible either on the logical plane or on the plane of experience and social praxis.

For my part, I hope that GRIC will one day seriously set about working on this problem so that it may suggest a new attitude to resolve this dilemma, which besets all our plural societies today.

Joseph Gelot, Tunis

The object of these few lines is simply to enunciate what I believe underlies some amendments I had suggested for the common text that were not adopted.

I quite agree with our common document's insistence that there is no "direct revelation," that revelation always presupposes a human mediation, that there is no "Word of God in the pure state" in the scriptures.

But we have not sufficiently stressed that this observation cannot be applied by a Christian in the same way to Christian revelation as to qur'anic revelation. Christians must take care fully to respect the mystery of the very *Person* of Jesus in the way they speak.

Jesus certainly expressed himself in human speech, and therefore in a language that was in itself inadequate for the total expression of the mystery of God. But— and this is the essential point—he is *the Word of God in Person*, the Word of the Father, and this is precisely why his human speech (human word of *the Word*), created to be sure and therefore surely limited, has such a *fulness* that it *alone* is capable of introducing humanity to the *fulness* of what we can only glimpse during the time of faith, of the mystery of God. The whole of John's Gospel is but a restatement of this.

It has been duly noted that the human words of Jesus are "theandric." The human words of the Qur'ān are not.

As to the origin of the latter, Christian faith can recognize a real influx of divine grace, and it can observe their revelatory bearing on the hearts of sincere believers. But they are not for all that "complementary" to the revelation in Jesus Christ, even if they offer different accents in the perception of the mystery of God. These accents can challenge Christian perception, but only as "factors of a revelation of the meaning of the revelation"; that is, by pushing the Christian believer, with the impulse of the Spirit, to a more authentic refocusing on the revelation in Jesus Christ, as Father Geffré has said so well.

This is to say that I do not consider myself a signatory to the commentary on the section entitled "Another Expression of the Word of God: A Common but Different Monotheism." The data analyzed are exact in themselves, but they have been given theological import that seems ambiguous to me.

Notes

INTRODUCTION

1. The French version of this work was published in Paris by the Editions du Centurion in 1987; translations into other languages, including Arabic, are in preparation.

2. There is a general description of GRIC in the review *Islamochristiana* (Rome, PISAI), 4 (1978): 175–86. The same review publishes each year an account of the GRIC general meetings. See also another description of GRIC in *Lumière et Vie* (Lyons), 163 (July-Aug. 1983): 81–85.

3. Reports from several of these colloquia have been published:

Rencontre islamo-chrétienne: *Conscience musulmane et conscience chrétienne aux prises avec les défis du développement*, Carthage-Hammamet-Kairouan, November 11–17, 1974, University of Tunis, CERES, Série Etudes islamiques no. 5; Tunis: CERES, 1976. (In Arabic: *Al-multaqā al-islāmī al-masīḥī: Al-ḍamīr al-masīḥī wa-l-ḍamīr al-islāmī fī muwājahati-hā li-taḥaddiyāt al-numū.*)

Rencontre islamo-chrétienne: *Sens et niveaux de la révélation*, Carthage, April 30-May 5, 1979, University of Tunis, CERES, Série Etudes islamiques no. 6; Tunis: CERES, 1980. (In Arabic: *Al-multaqā al-masīḥī al-islāmī al-ṯānī: Ma'ānī al-waḥy wa-l-tanzīl wa-mustawayyāti-hā.*)

Rencontre islamo-chrétienne: *Islam, christianisme et Droits de l'Homme*, Amilcar, Carthage, May 24–29, 1982. Tunis, CERES, 1985. (In Arabic: *Al-multaqā al-islāmī al-masīḥī al-ṯāliṯ. Al-islām wa-l-masīḥiyya wa-ḥuqūq al-insān.*)

There is an analytical list of various recent international Muslim-Christian colloquia in Maurice Borrmans's, *Orientations pour un dialogue entre chrétiens et musulmans* (Paris: Cerf, 1981), pp. 175–79. More detailed is Borrmans's "Le dialogue islamo-chrétien depuis dix ans," *Pro Mundi Vita* (Brussels), 74 (Sept.-Oct. 1978). For a similar work in the World Council of Churches, see J. B. Taylor, ed. *Christians Meeting Muslims: WCC Papers on Ten Years of Christian-Muslim Dialogue* (Geneva: WCC, 1977).

4. It is this private character, unofficial and therefore nonrepresentative, which explains why we have never sought to have representatives within GRIC of the various currents or churches of our two religions. The only criteria were the competence and willingness to engage in common research. But without seeking to do so, GRIC has included Catholic, Orthodox, and Protestant Christians as well as Sunni and Shi'ite Muslims.

5. The original was in French. The English rendition (edited) by Michael Fitzgerald is taken from *Islamochristiana*, 6 (1980): 230–33. The Arabic version, by Tariq Mitri, is in *Islamochristiana* 10 (1984): 20–24 of the Arabic section.

6. Part of this work appeared under the title "Religion et État" in *Islamochristiana* 12 (1986).

7. Experience has shown the need for GRIC to obtain some sort of official recognition, especially in order to receive and manage the subsidies received from various Christian and Muslim organizations. These sums allow us to function, mainly by covering travel costs for the annual meetings. For this reason GRIC was registered as an association under the French law of July 1, 1901 (*JORF*, October 13, 1982), with its head office in Paris: 20 rue du Printemps, 75017 Paris. Further information or documents may be obtained from the general secretary: Michel Lelong, 35 av. Georges Clemenceau, F–94700 Maisons-Alfort. Applications for similar status are pending for those sections where registration has been deemed necessary or useful.

CHAPTER 1

1. Besides, the theologians must treat this as an effect of the will of God, who could have chosen another means of communication.

2. Note, for example, the convenient opposition in the biblical text between a level of discourse based on self-understanding (e.g., "God said to Moses") and one based on reflection (e.g., "Jesus said that because he knew what was in people's hearts"), which offers a possible tool for comparing scriptural idioms.

3. The traditional interpretation, that has been made sacred, can acquire a status that is almost equal to that of the foundational book.

4. The degree of awareness of the interpretive factor in any reading constitutes a criterion of classification. Between the verbatim repetition of revelation (which could be understood as a simple perpetuation of the sense) and the type of inquiry that utilizes a complex conceptual instrumentation in order to reply, for example, to questions of contingency ("in which circumstances," "in which language," etc., was the first discourse revealed? "Why, when, by whom, how has it been assembled, transcribed?"), there is a range of dependency on grammar, history, and other elements of information.

CHAPTER 3

1. We will not here repeat the whole inquiry into this vast subject, for it lasted several years. The third part, which concerns the general history of Christian tradition, would by itself exceed the limits of our publication. A detailed exposition can be found in a series of articles in the review *Islamochristiana* (Rome, PISAI), beginning with no. 8 (1982). Here we shall give only a brief summary.

2. G. Khodr, "Le christianisme dans un monde devenu pluraliste: l'économie de l'Esprit Saint," *Irenikon*, 1972: 191–202.

3. There is a critical and nearly exhaustive bibliography of these writings, and the whole corpus of literature on Islamo-Christian confrontation from its beginnings (7th century) in the review *Islamochristiana* (Rome: PISAI). This has included in each of its yearly issues (since its foundation in 1975) a systematic bibliography of this literature, Christian and Muslim, in Arabic, Greek, Syriac, Latin, Armenian, etc., in chronological order: "Bibliography of Muslim-Christian Dialogue."

4. See the critical edition of the Arabic rendition of this dialogue (the original

was in Syriac), with a French translation in *Islamochristiana*, 3 (1977): 107–75. The passage on Muhammad is on pp. 150–52 (Arabic) and 173–75 (French).

5. See the critical edition of this letter (Arabic text and French translation in Paul Khoury, *Paul d'Antioche, évêque melkite de Sidon (XIIe s.)* (Beirut: Recherches de l'ILO, 24, 1964), French and Arabic; the reference here is to pp. 59–83 (Arabic) and 169–87 (French).

6. The best overviews of this literature are the books of Adel-Théodore Khoury, *Les théologiens byzantins et l'islam, textes et auteurs (VIIIe-XIIIe s).* (Louvain-Paris, 1969), and *Polémique byzantine contre l'islam (VIIIe-XIIIe s.)* (Leiden: Brill, 1972).

7. The best overview of the image of Islam in the medieval West is by N. Daniel, *Islam and the West: The Making of an Image* (Edinburgh University Press, 1960). It needs to be supplemented. See also Simon Jargy, *Islam et chrétienté: Les fils d'Abraham entre la confrontation et le dialogue* (Geneva: Labor et Fides, 1981), pp. 103–29; Maxime Rodinson, *La fascination de l'islam: Les étapes du regard occidental sur le monde musulman* (Paris: Maspéro, 1982), pp. 17–106; P. Senac, *L'image de l'autre: histoire de l'Occident médiéval face à l'Islam* (Paris: Flammarion, 1983); J. J. Waardenburg, *L'Islam dans le miroir de l'Occident* (Paris-The Hague: Mouton, 1963); Jean-Marie Gaudeul, *Encounters and Clashes: Islam and Christianity in History* (Rome: PISAI, 1984), 2 vols. For the reformation and the modern era, consult especially V. Segesvary, *L'Islam et la Réforme* (Lausanne: L'Age d'Homme, 1978); Y. Moubarac, *Recherches sur la pensée chrétienne et l'Islam dans les temps modernes et à l'époque contemporaine* (Beirut: Cénacle libanais, 1977); see also Rodinson, Fascination, and Waardenburg, *L'Islam.*

8. See C. Courtois, "Grégoire VII et l'Afrique du Nord," *Revue historique*, 2 (1945): 92–122, 193–225.

9. The title he gave to his study of Ibn Arabi is revealing: *El Islam Cristianizado* (Madrid, 1931); also for Ghāzalī: *La espiritualidad de Algazel y su sentido cristiano*, 3 vols. (Madrid, 1934–40).

10. See the stimulating study by Lucie Pruvost, "From Tolerance to Spiritual Emulation: An Analysis of Official Texts on Christian-Muslim Dialogue," *Islamochristiana* 6 (1980): 1–9; P. Rossano, "Les grands documents de l'Eglise catholique au sujet des musulmans," ibid., 8 (1982): 13–23; and the recent work of Michel Lelong, *L'Eglise nous parle de l'Islam: du concile à Jean-Paul II* (Paris: Chalet, 1982).

11. Since this text was edited, a new summit has been reached during the pope's visit to Casablanca (August 19, 1985) with the remarkable texts in French in *Documentation catholique*, 1903 (October 6, 1985): 940–46; in French, English, and Arabic in *Islamochristiana* 11 (1985): 191–209.

12. French text in *Documentation catholique*, 1720 (May 15, 1977): 480–83.

13. For this entire historical section, there are many details and references in Robert Caspar, *Traité de théologie musulmane*, 3rd ed. (Rome: PISAI, 1986), pp. 75–116; we have greatly benefited from this work in preparing this summary.

14. See St. Thomas Aquinas, *Summa theologica*, IIa-IIae, Prophecy, q. 172, art. 4: the distinction between sanctifying grace (*gratum faciens*) and the free gift to the community (*gratis data*).

15. *Summa theologica*, IIa-IIae, q. 1, art. 2, ad 2.

16. *Summa theologica*, IIa-IIae, q. 170–74, esp. q. 174, art. 6.

17. Charles Ledit, *Mahomet, Israël et le Christ* (Paris: La Colombe, 1956), pp. 160–74.

18. He made this suggestion during the third "Journées romaines" in 1960. See

Rapport sur les "Journées romaines," 1960, mimeographed. See the summary of his address, "Prolégomènes ecclésiologiques," p. 3: "If Muhammad had first been turned away from paganism and directed toward monotheism by some prophetic gift, it could only be a partial and extracanonical prophethood that enabled him to block his personal opinions." This "partial prophetic light" recalls one of Louis Massignon's phrases in a letter to a colleague: "Muhammad is enlightened on certain points but not on others." Text in R. Charles-Barzel, *O Vierge puissante* (Paris: La Colombe, 1958), pp. 58–61.

19. Yves Congar, *Vraie et fausse réforme dans l'Eglise* (Paris: Cerf, 1950), pp. 196–228.

20. Robert Caspar, *Cours de théologie musulmane,* 1st ed., mimeographed (La Manouba, 1960), pp. 48–50. In later editions of the *Cours* this position was abandoned.

21. See the decree against modernism, *Lamentabili,* 1907 (Denz.-Schönm., 2021/3421). This was considered in a more general way by the Second Vatican Council (*Dei Verbum,* 4).

22. See *Rencontre islamo-chrétienne: Sens et niveaux de la révélation: Carthage, 30 avril–5 mai 1979* (Tunis: CERES, 1980), Série Etudes islamiques no. 6; pp. 249–51.

23. This is the formulation of the Vatican II text that considers the Muslim faith: *Declaration on the Relations of the Church to Non-Christian Religions (Nostra Aetate),* no. 3.

24. For example, Claude Geffré in his article, "Le Coran, une Parole de Dieu différente?," *Lumière et Vie,* 163 (July-Aug. 1983): 21–32.

25. Robert Caspar, *Traité de théologie musulmane,* pp. 98–100.

26. On the doctrinal approach to Christianity taken by the Qur'ān and Islam, see Robert Caspar, "La rencontre des théologies," *Lumière et Vie,* 163, (July-Aug. 1983): 63–80.

27. Soteriology: with regard to the message of salvation in the gospel.

28. This is the theme and conclusion of the book by Christian Duquoc, *Dieu différent* (Paris: Cerf, 1977), see esp. pp. 138–48: "Le Dieu de Jésus et les religions."

29. According to classical Islamic doctrines, the conditions for being a *'ālim mujtahid* (a scholar offering a personal opinion) have essentially been an intimate knowledge of the roots (*uṣūl*) of religion: Qur'ān, *hadith,* opinions of the major authors, etc., and an aptitude for reasoning by analogy. The *mujtahid* was contrasted with the *muqallid* (blind imitator); the question of *ijtihād* (personal reflection) has been hotly debated, and no agreement was established about the conditions and methods of *ijtihād.* Its first theoretician, the Imam al-Shāfi'ī (2nd/8th century) defined it by the use of *qiyās* (reason by analogy) in questions on which there was no clear text in the Qur'ān and *hadith.* But Ibn Hazm (5th/11th century) rejected *qiyās,* whereas Ibn Rushd, the grandfather of Averroes (6th/12th century), found it inadequate. With the decline in Muslim thought, *ijtihād* was generally supplanted by *taqlīd.* Since the "renaissance" of the past two centuries, the theory of *ijtihād* has been profoundly revised in the new context of the Muslim world. Today, the conditions and methods of *ijtihād* can be set forth as follows:

1. It should bring a critical examination of the theoretical and judicial legacy of the past, which is only a human construction to which time has given an aura of sanctity.

2. It should pull free from literal interpretations of the texts, especially the

qur'anic text, and draw inspiration from its spirit in order to elaborate new solutions appropriate to our own age.

3. Instead of becoming polarized over the judicial aspects or socio-political implications of Islam, it should see Islam above all as a witness before God and before conscience.

4. It should base itself on the principle of individual responsibility and refrain from claims of legislating in the name of God.

5. It should respect human rights without reservation, including the freedom of conscience and belief, the right to bodily wholeness of all persons (including delinquents), equality of rights and duties between men and women, etc.

6. It should respect the principles of freedom of expression and ideological pluralism as rights inherent in the human person and factors of encounter that radiate light.

7. It should pull free from apologetic and polemic reflexes and prolix discourse on "authenticity" in order to face without fear the problems of the present and the future.

See 'Abd al-Majīd al-Sharfī, "Definitions of *ijtihād* among Muslim jurists and theologians," paper presented (in Arabic) at the colloquium on *ijtihād*, University of Tunis, 1985.

30. There was not enough time for the Muslim editors of the Tunis group to complete the planned inquiry described here. In practical terms, they only did the study of the Qur'ān. So the reader will not find in this text any equivalent of the long historical examination of the Christian view of the Qur'ān, which would have presented the history of Muslim thinking about the Bible and Christianity. Elements of this history are to be found in the works cited in relation to the history of the Christian attitudes to Islam, for many of these treat both Muslim and Christian sides of the story. Scientific studies of this history by Muslims are still rare. We should note in particular Abd al-Majid al-Sharfi, "Al-fikr al-islāmī fil-radd 'alā l-nasārā ilā nihāyat al-qarn al-rābi [Islamic thought on the refutation of Christians up to the end of the fourth/tenth century], doctoral thesis presented to the University of Tunis, 1982 (Tunis: MTE, 1986). A French translation is planned.

31. On the famous *mubāhala*, see L. Massignon in *Opera Minora*, 1: 550–67, and A. Meziane in *Islamochristiana*, 2 (1976): 59–67.

32. The term *taḥrīf* comes from the root ḤRF, "side." It would therefore suggest approaching the side and deviating from the right way.

33. "Foi d'Abraham et foi islamique," in *Islamochristiana*, 5 (1979): 2.

34. See esp. R. Caspar and J. M. Gaudeul, "Textes de la Tradition musulmane concernant le *taḥrīf* (falsification) des Ecritures," *Islamochristiana*, 6 (1980): 61–104. Our text summarizes the principal conclusions of this article.

35. This is a principle of Muslim jurisprudence (*fiqh*), which recommends the renunciation of a practice that is in itself legitimate but open to misinterpretation by simple minds. In the case at hand, the title "son of God" would be permissible as a metaphor, but it is dangerous because it could be taken literally.

36. The evidence of such opinions on the death of Jesus on the cross before his "elevation" is to be found in the earliest *tafsīr*s, especially that of Tabari (d. 311/923): "dead for three hours"; see the texts on Qur'ān 3:52 and 4:156. See 'Abd al-Majīd al-Sharfī, "Al-masīhiyyah fi tafsīr al-Tabarī," in *Revue tunisienne des sciences sociales*, 58–59 (1979): 53–96. This article has been translated into English: "Christianity in the Qur'ān Commentary of Tabari" in *Islamochristiana*, 6 (1980): 105–48,

here 125. Other authors, especially Isma'ilis and the philosophico-mystical encyclopedia of the "Brothers of Purity" (*Ikhwān al-Ṣafā'*) (4th/10th century) argued that the "humanity" (*nāsūt*) of Jesus had indeed been crucified. See Y. Marquet, "Les Ikhwān al-Ṣafā' et le christianisme" in *Islamochristiana*, 8 (1982): 128–58, here 145–47 and 159, with reference to the *Rasa'il* and other studies. Texts translated into French by M. Hayek, *Le Christ et l'islam* (Paris, 1959), pp. 128–32, 227–32. Tabari noted that this was "the opinion of most of the *falāsifah* (Islamic philosophers)." In fact, this is easy enough to understand. For these neoplatonic philosophers, the human being is a soul imprisoned in a material body: killing the body (on the cross in Jesus' case) is not killing the soul, but liberating the soul from its prison.

37. Notably the docetist gnostic school: Jesus is God and only "apparently" human.

38. Muslim literature about this quest for indications of the proclamation of Muhammad in the actual text of the Bible is voluminous and repetitive. The biblical passages most often invoked are, in the Old Testament, first of all Deut. 18:15 and 18, where Moses announces to the people of Israel that "the Lord will raise up for you . . . *from among your brothers a prophet like me,*" with the following argument: the "brothers" of the people of Israel are the Arabs, so the "prophet like Moses" whom God will raise up can only be Muhammad. Let us remember that this same text provided the Christians' principal argument for the proclamation of Jesus as Messiah: see Acts 3:22; 7:25, 37, etc. Then there is a series of messianic texts: Isa. 5:26–30; 9:5; Dan. 2:37–45; Hab. 3:3–7; etc. For the New Testament, attention focuses on eschatological texts, like the sending of the son to the faithless vineyard workers (Matt. 21:33–46) or the acclamation: "Blessed is the one who comes/will come in the name of the Lord!" (Matt. 23:39) and especially the proclamation of the sending of the Paraclete, "who will proclaim all truth to you" (John 13:31; 14:31; 15:26; 16:7, 13. We do not consider the text called "Gospel of Barnabas" (*Injīl Barnābā*), which has much to say about Jesus' proclamation of Muhammad, for this is an apocryphal writing compiled no earlier than the sixteenth century. But as such it is a good representative of this Islamic apologetic tradition. On this problem, see inter alios M. de Epalza, "Le milieu hispano-moresque de l'Evangile islamisant de Barnabé (XVIᵉ-XVIIᵉ siècles)" in *Islamochristiana*, 8 (1982): 159–83, with references to the earlier studies by J. Jomier, J. Slomp, and the version of the manuscript in Venetian dialect published by L. Cirillo and M. Frémaux (Paris, 1977).

39. For example, the Socinians and the Unitarian branch of Protestantism, and, recently, the works of the Protestant theologians Norman Pittinger, John B. Cobb, Jr., and others, and the Roman Catholics Georges Morel, Jean Moussé, and others. See also John Hick, "A Recent Development within Christian Monotheism," paper read to the international symposium of the International Progress Organization, held at Rome, November 17–19, 1981, published in Hans Kochler, ed. *The Concept of Monotheism in Islam and Christianity* (Vienna: Braumüller, 1982).

40. For Muslims, the message transmitted by the "gospel" of the historical Jesus is "pure Christianity," which is a component of Islam, just as Christianity claims to have subsumed the pure religion of Israel. By contrast, the Christian dogmas (Trinity, incarnation) are posterior elaborations, which Islam rejects.

41. On this subject see "L'Islam et les religions nonmusulmanes; quelques textes positifs," *Islamochristiana*, 3 (1977): 39–63. The authors mentioned are the Ikhwan al-Ṣafā', Ghazālī, Muhammad 'Abduh, Kamel Ḥusayn; the list could be extended.

42. Or a Muslim, we could add, although the *hadith* seems to identify *islam* with *fiṭra* (human nature).

CONCLUSION

1. One could develop an impression of this by consulting the reports of the annual assemblies. These are available from the GRIC Secretariat: Michel Lelong, 35 avenue Georges Clemenceau, F-94700 Maisons-Alfort, France.

2. The mu'tazili theologian al-Iskafī (3rd/9th century) affirmed that "God does not speak, but causes speech." Quoted by Khayyat, *Kitāb al-intiṣār*, Nybert edition (Cairo, 1925), p. 57; Nader edition (Beirut, 1957), p. 48. Some see this awareness of the distance between the Qur'ān as Word of God and its written expression to be at the root of the famous mu'tazili distinction between the uncreated Qur'ān and the created Qur'ān; this distinction was taken up by ibādi theology and, in modern times, by the great reformist Muhammad 'Abduh (d. 1905).

Index